Meditations From Iraq

A Chaplain's Ministry In The Middle East
2003-2004

Chaplain (LTC) Lance Kittleson
United States Army Reserve
3d Corps Support Command (CA)

CSS Publishing Company, Inc., Lima, Ohio

MEDITATIONS FROM IRAQ

Scripture quotations marked (NIV) are from the Holy Bible, New International Version.
Copyright © 1973, 1978, 1984 International Bible Society. Used by permission of
Zondervan Bible Publishers. All rights reserved.

Scripture quotations marked (GNB) are from the Good News Bible in Today's English
Version. Copyright © American Bible Society 1966, 1971, 1976. Used by permission.

Scripture quotations marked (The Message) are from The Message by Eugene H. Peterson,
copyright © 1993, 1994, 1995, 1996, 2000, 2001, 2002. Used by permission of NavPress
Publishing Group. All rights reserved.

Scripture quotations marked (NRSV) are from the New Revised Standard Version of the
Bible, copyright 1989 by the Division of Christian Education of the National Council of
the Churches of Christ in the USA. Used by permission

Library of Congress Cataloging-in-Publication Data

Kittleson, Lance, 1951-
    Meditations from Iraq : a chaplain's ministry in the Middle East, 2003-2004 / Lance
Kittleson.
       p. cm.
       ISBN 0-7880-2345-4 (perfect bound : alk. paper)
  1. Meditations. 2. Iraq War, 2003—Religious aspects—Christianity—Meditations. I. Title.

BV4897.W2K58 2004
270.8'3'09—dc22

                                                                              2004022193

For more information about CSS Publishing Company resources, visit our website at
www.csspub.com or e-mail us at custserv@csspub.com or call (800) 241-4056.

Cover design by Chris Patton
ISBN 0-7880-2345-4   PRINTED IN U.S.A.

To my father, CSM (Ret.) Galen Kittleson,
a true soldier's soldier and warrior,
and my mother, Darlene,
a soldier's spouse who had the hardest job of all,
watching and waiting as her husband and son went off to war.

To my wife, Gail,
who knows what it means to wait, hope, and pray
from 7,000 miles away.

Table Of Contents

Preface

The e-mails from Lance Kittleson first appeared in the church newsletter last spring. The newsletter editor for our little rural congregation asked if I minded if she included an e-mail that Lance had sent to his mother. I cried as I read "A Baptism In The Desert." There was that moment of instant recognition. Lance was telling a story of faith from a pastor's point of view. As a general category of books, a pastor's story is not too unusual. There are many books available which fit this description. The familiar story of one pastor was not what caught my attention that April afternoon. What I heard was the voice of a pastor ministering under amazing conditions at the edge of war.

I experienced the power of God's grace in two ways as I have continued to read these e-mails from the chaplain. First, I heard the story of faith of an ordinary parish pastor who served God in a rather extraordinary setting. Lance would be the first to insist that he is nothing special. Such humility is appropriate to a parish pastor. In other times, Lance would probably be sitting in the church office, reading over his sermon, praying for the people, having supper at home with his wife Gail.

But, these are not ordinary times for many ordinary people like Lance. Instead of that church office in the midwest, Lance sits in dusty tents, gathers around packing crate altars, and shares the sacraments of God's grace and love with men and women who are also a long way from their families and their homes. Lance answered God's call to a congregation that moves along in trucks, carries gas masks, and faces death each day. Lance's faithful ministry for God in these circumstances makes him an unusual pastor with a unique congregation.

The second thing that I experienced in these e-mails is the power of God to make the ordinary precious. These letters are filled with simple moments of serving coffee and serving God, baptism by bottled water and denominational tensions melting under a desert sun. People do not carry rifles into the worship services in my church, but they do at the Sunday services that Lance directs. People do not come to church worried about gas attacks,

7

but they do with Lance's congregation. The people of my congregation share prayers for safety for soldiers because Lance and his soldiers work for peace on earth.

I knew the minute I began to read the letters that they needed to be shared with others. God's Word comes to all of us new and fresh as we read "R.H.I.P. (Rank Has Its Privileges) Servants" and "Saint SGT Murphy." We can experience and share some of that freshness that God's children in a desert in Iraq find through the work of the chaplains to the Armed Forces. Lance shares with all of us a small piece of God's kingdom in a far-off land.

Reverend Doctor Elaine Siemsen
St. Olaf College, Northfield, Minnesota
St. Peter Lutheran Church, Toeterville, Iowa

Foreword

Waiting. That's not on my list of favorite pastimes. But, lately I've done lots of it. This advent has special meaning for me. My husband, Lance, has been deployed as a chaplain with the U.S. Army in Iraq since January. Originally his unit was to have been home by Christmas. Now the time has been extended until February or March.

The first five months of his absence weren't pleasant. But, I knew he was the perfect person to be in Iraq to help young soldiers through the war. He was challenged and purposeful, and that was satisfying to me. During this time our daughter began having problems with her pregnancy and was put on bed rest. I went to be with her, and it was the most difficult period of Lance's deployment. The heat and humidity in Hawaii were hard on my body, and I spent my time waiting — waiting for yet another happening.

Our first grandchild, Eli, was in no hurry to enter the world. My daughter and I kept trying to find air-conditioned places to spend the hottest part of the days as we were waiting, trying to fill the time as creatively as possible.

One day, after reading Mark's story of Jesus walking on water, I made this journal entry, "You know how impatience stalks my joy, Lord. This day I especially need a sense of your presence, holding my hand as I wait. Empower me with your peace out here with you in the waves. Encourage me with your touch. Strengthen me against the tides of loneliness and inertia that would drag me down."

As we knew he would, Eli captivated all our hearts when he entered the world. Our only regret is that Lance can't enjoy these first weeks with him. This is just one of several important life transitions Lance has missed during the past nine months, including our daughter's college graduation, and our twenty-fifth wedding anniversary.

The whole scenario gives new meaning to the *Advent*. We wait in hope. After 25 years of marriage, there's no question that our relationship is worth the wait. Isn't this what the coming of Jesus is about? God wants a relationship with us. God comes as a human

9

being so we can relate to him. God comes in the form of Jesus —
just as surely as our new little grandson came, and there's no doubt
about it: The relationship is definitely worth the wait.

Gail Kittleson, Advent 2003

Author's Preface

Forbes Field, Topeka, Kansas, was never such a sweet sight on a cold Valentine's Day, 2004, even though it was 1:12 a.m. and my wife was 500 miles away in Iowa.

The Continental Airline charter jet that had lifted off from Kuwait City International Airport with shouts of joy touched down after an eighteen-hour flight, thus ending a year in the combat zone called Kuwait and Iraq for myself and the 138 other Army Reserve soldiers of the 3d Corps Support Command, a unit from Des Moines, Iowa, comprised of citizen-soldiers hailing from Iowa and at least six other surrounding states and even from as far away as Oregon and Alberta, Canada.

Our journey took us from Iowa to Germany to Kuwait to Iraq and finally Kansas before arriving back in Des Moines to a wonderful "Welcome Home" from family and friends. It was, as they say, one of those experiences you're glad you did, but wouldn't give a nickel to do again.

These stories and meditations from that year away from America were never intended to be compiled and made into a book. They began simply as e-mails from Kuwait and Iraq to my family, present and former congregations, and the unit's Family Readiness Group meant to communicate what life was like for us overseas. Producing a book never crossed my mind while trudging through sand and sandstorms, sprinting for SCUD bunkers, worshiping in a stifling tent, battling the Kuwaiti crud, traveling along Iraqi roads on the lookout for roadside ambushes and RPG attacks, or standing in hot dusty lines for food seeking to do ministry in the mundane and exciting moments of war 7,000 miles from home. The vast majority of the time, it was anything but dangerous for me.

These stories were written simply out of my pastoral, almost innate, need to write and illustrate truths of life and faith even when in uniform and far from a *normal* civilian congregation back home. Over twenty years as a Lutheran parish pastor and 27 years in uniform as a Reservist and Active duty soldier, apparently etched strong patterns into my neural pathways demanding that I always be alert for illustrations and sermon material wherever they may be found.

On most observations, I pulled out of the leg pocket of my faded, dust- and sweat-soaked desert camouflage uniform, my battered, but trusty, free notepad from Dralle's Department Store in Greene, Iowa, and recorded the germinal thought for most of the meditations that were later fleshed out on paper, typed into a computer, and e-mailed to my English-teacher spouse. After her usual gargantuan task of making grammatical and style corrections, they were sent out from Iraq to those who might have an interest and became for me what personal diaries are to most other people.

The surprising thing to me was that others actually read them and responded positively.

Certainly, this was due to the instinctive need of families back home to receive as much information as possible about the condition and life of their loved ones in a combat zone. The uncertainty and unknowns of war dictated this hunger. Although I did not deliberately send these stories to unit soldiers, occasionally some did make their way back to them and in a small way seemed to express some of their experiences and emotions from a very significant and dangerous episode of their lives. For that I am grateful to God.

Yet, publishing these thoughts comes only with much trepidation and at the encouragement of many. Only reluctantly I supersede my Norwegian piety that dictates that this is far too pretentious for a small town parish pastor to believe his words are of value to others outside the pulpit.

With this in mind, a caution is required. This is the experience of just one chaplain among hundreds in the Middle East and one soldier among over a hundred thousand in the Central Theater of Operations, many of whom found themselves in far more dangerous and difficult situations and ministry than I.

The 3d Corps Support Command's mission was not to "close with and destroy the enemy or his capacity to resist" — the classic military definition of combat arms soldiers. This headquarter's objective was to insure that those Americans who did meet the enemy face-to-face had the equipment, ammunition, food, and supplies to do so. This was a not a combat unit where war's ugliness and death is seen up close on a daily and regular basis.

These meditations do not purport to be indicative of the experience for all soldiers in Iraq and Kuwait, nor do they seek to examine the morality of war, in general, and this conflict, in particular, with all of its ambiguities. They simply reflect my observations and thoughts as an activated Army Reserve soldier and chaplain in whatever circumstances I found myself as a member of my unit.

My prayer and desire is that whatever good results from these pages may honor the Americans serving their nation around the world, their even braver loved ones and families back home who have sacrificed as much if not more than their soldier, and ultimately draw the reader to the gracious and loving Savior, Jesus Christ who walks with his people in war and peace or wherever this life takes them.

I gratefully thank my wife, Gail, for her constant encouragement and editing skills and Pat Boysen, the leader of the 3d COSCOM Family Readiness Group in Des Moines, Iowa, who faithfully passed on these thoughts from Iraq with ample encouragement to the families and friends of the Army Reserve family.

Chaplain [LTC] Lance Kittleson
March 31, 2004
Mason City, Iowa

A Baptism In The Desert

The message on the board outside the chapel of Camp Virginia, Kuwait, besides announcing the religious schedule for today was an oft-used quote of a seventeenth-century English soldier about to go into battle. He said, "Lord, thou knowest how busy I must be this day. If I forget thee, do not thou forget me." These are words spoken by a soldier to soldiers of every era. There are many of them here in the desert of Kuwait waiting the unleashing of "the dogs of war." It will no doubt be soon, as the pace and intensity of everyone's life increases in proportion to the approach of the order to "cross the line of departure and attack." Camp Virginia is a sprawling base with dusty, wind-blown sand and not a tree in sight; just the kind of place the Army seems to love to put its soldiers.

As war approaches, so does the contemplation of many soldiers' souls. Today, a young female soldier comes to be baptized at the large tent that serves as the camp chapel. A briefing by a commander to his leaders about the impending operation takes place on one side of the chapel while I, the camp pastor, and the soldier are by the altar at the other. The altar is two cobbled wooden shipping crates with no paraments. (The last altar was permanently *borrowed* and has not reappeared. We dug the crates out of the dump and put them together. "Adapt and Overcome" the troops say.) At the altar, I quietly read Ephesians 2:8, 9 to the soldier in her battle-dress uniform.

We'd talked several days before when she came into the chapel and asked to speak with a chaplain about her fears, her background, and her many sorrows, including the sorrow of the pastor from her home church telling her she was not worthy to be baptized in Jesus' name, that she was not pure enough. Apparently in that tradition, baptism is a reward for good behavior and not a gift of God's grace. But on the eve of war, this young trooper wanted to know that Jesus was *for her* and not *against her* and wanted to be part of his family. My Lutheran hackles rose and I announced to her that where I come from, baptism is a gift of God and none of us can ever be good enough for it.

I read to her the words of God through Saint Paul (NIV), "For it is by grace you have been saved, through faith — and this not from yourselves, it is the gift of God — not by works, so that no one can boast" (Ephesians 2:8-9) Looking into her eyes, I quietly said, "This is God's gift to you because he has always loved you. He will never love you more or less than he already does." Then, in perhaps the most unique baptism I have ever done in over twenty years of ordination, with no font and only a congregation of quizzical on-looking commanders and staff officers, I poured the promise of God in Christ out on her head from a liter container of bottled water.

Three times the water of grace flowed off her head, down her cheeks, mixing with her own tears flowing onto her uniform and splashing onto the chapel floor. Wiping her head with my red "farmer" bandana, the words "You have been sealed by the Holy Spirit and marked with the cross of Christ forever" were spoken over this new member of God's family even while the baptismal water was quickly drying up on the plywood floor as the desert sun reached its zenith. But, I knew that God's grace would never dry up in the baptized believer's life and certainly not in this young soldier's heart.

As I put on my Kevlar helmet with desert camo and a cross sewed on the front, snapping on the web gear, grabbing my ICE pack (Individual Chemical Equipment) that goes with the gas mask that never leaves a modern day soldier's side, and prepared to trudge through the dusty streets of Camp Virginia in the "wilderness" of Kuwait, I can't help but think that like that gas mask, God's Spirit will go with that young soldier everywhere this life takes her as she, too, leaves the chapel. "Never will I leave you or forsake" God promises. Waddling along with my 25 pounds of equipment, I carry a liter of bottled water, taking a good gulp every few 100 meters and it is only down the road that I realize I'm drinking from the same bottle of water that just baptized a new child of God.

Maybe that, too, is a parallel of the believer's life in Christ. Baptism is a one-time event, but it is also a daily gulping of the gift of God's love as we trudge through our own deserts of life —

16

whether in Kuwait on the eve of war or in our own joys, sorrows, struggles, and busyness in the mountains of Oregon, the corn and bean fields of Iowa, or wherever God's people may find themselves. In taking those gulps of daily grace we can be assured that no matter what our battles may be, God will never forget us or forsake his children of grace through faith in Jesus Christ, our Lord.

The Odd Couple

"The body of Christ broken for your sins," croaked one voice. "The blood of Christ shed for you," croaked another.

The formula was repeated over and over as each came, weapons slung over their shoulder or safely strapped into their shoulder holster. They formed a long line down the center aisle of this makeshift Army chapel in the desert of Kuwait. They came to the altar consisting of two packing crates nailed together to receive the elements of Holy Communion and to taste God's presence and grace from an odd couple of Army chaplains.

"The body of Christ" spoken by a southern Baptist with a Georgia drawl made even more soft and mellow by the Kuwaiti dust (*crud* as the soldiers call the respiratory illness that plagues virtually everyone here); "The blood of Christ" spoken by a midwestern Lutheran croaking out the words through the lingering effects of the same crud and runny nose. But, none of these soldiers in the generated-lighted tent seemed to care that a Baptist and a Lutheran were offering them the Lord's Supper. Theological and liturgical correctness took a back seat that night to something that was far more important to them.

They came to taste the promise and presence of God, not to argue over the meaning of the sacrament like they were at a Sunday evening barbecue with nothing better to do. They came to dip the bread into the wine so they could, by faith, taste a connectedness rather than correctness, a connectedness to the Savior, his presence, his gift of love and life.

This was no theoretical exercise for these troops in desert camouflage. The war has been rumbling on for several weeks now. Most of these soldiers would never hear a shot fired in anger, though perhaps they would witness a Patriot missile fired at an incoming SCUD. Love and life are no longer taken for granted as the young in particular are wont to do. The self-confidence in their soldiering, their cause, their country is still there, but it has been tempered by the casualties, the Missing in Action, the POWs that combat brings. War that was always remote and a training exercise has become less clinical and more real. They now realize it is not some other generation that must go into battle. It is their turn, here, now.

Faith no longer is an academic exercise as they contemplate the days ahead. It must either be real and palpable, now, or it will never be of value.

Yet, they are not unique in this hunger for a "real and present God." Their elders are no different when the diagnosis is cancer and the prognosis is not good; or when the accident brings the middle of the night dreaded phone call; or the family is falling apart and there seems nothing that can be done to stop it. We all run for assurance and hope and no pious, but theoretical, ivory tower faith will do. They want, and need, a strong connectedness to God; a faith for the brutish and horrible side of our lives as well as for the easier, good times. Surely, God understood that fact as he allowed his Son's body to be broken and his blood shed in the unspeakable horror of the cross.

These soldiers seem to understand it now more than ever in the face of war. They come down the plywood aisle of the chapel seeking a presence that will never abandon them nor leave them when life does its worst, when life *is* at its worst. They come shuffling in their brown desert boots, holding a hand out to receive the bread, and then to dip it into the wine. Some are clearly familiar with this method of communion; others are not; some make the sign of the cross as they take the elements into their body and soul, and others say "Amen" while still others quietly take it and return to their folding chair. They come and hear powerful words from the two old, croaking chaplain voices. "Broken *for you*, shed *for you*."

And the miracle happens.

Somehow, in the mystery of faith, somehow in God's promises of victory in the death and resurrection of his Son, somehow in our Lord's enduring promise in the bread and the wine, somehow a soldier's soul is sustained for whatever lies ahead. Weapons clatter against metal chairs as each returns to their seat, moving and adjusting the omnipresent gas mask around each soldier's hip in order to refit everyone into their seats. Then, the blessing following Holy Communion learned long ago flows from the chaplain's mouth, "Now may the body and blood of our Lord Jesus Christ strengthen and preserve you to eternal life. Go in peace and serve the Lord."

Go in peace seems so odd to say to soldiers in the midst of a war, but it is true, nonetheless. A soldier's soul is no different than a civilian's when they go into life's battles. Maybe it is the operating room for that less than fifty-fifty chance of survival, or the chemotherapy that may or may not do its hoped-for task, or any other difficult challenge in life when the outcome is anything but guaranteed to be what is hoped and prayed for.

Peace is what God gives to his children in the tumultuous and unknowable times of our lives. For in the hearing and believing: "The body of Christ broken *for you*, the blood of Christ shed *for you*." God comes, strengthens, and preserves us in his love wherever life takes us because that is why God sent his Son — that nothing might ever again separate his forgiven children from his gracious love.

Connectedness, not correctness.

How strange, and yet how wonderful, that God could, and would, use a Baptist and a Lutheran, two croaking old chaplains, a Holy Communion "Odd Couple" to offer his peace, assurance, and presence to soldiers in war. Our gracious God does all this and more by using common, earthly elements and simple, familiar words that begin in Christ and end in *for you* to any and all who would dare to believe these words: "The body of Christ broken *for you*. The blood of Christ shed *for you*."

Go in peace — even in war.

Dust To Dust

Earth to earth, ashes to ashes, dust to dust.
— Lutheran Book Of Worship

How many times had I spoken those words over parishioners, friends, and acquaintances as the last official words of the community of a faith over the mortal remains of one of its own?

The committal service of the Lutheran church is brief, based on centuries of tradition; words that have been spoken over countless caskets, in countless cemeteries, in countless places around the world.

"Earth to earth, ashes to ashes, dust to dust." These words have a different meaning out here in the Kuwaiti desert at camps where American troops gather to await equipment, orders, and missions that will send them off to the north to do their part in the war and in the rebuilding of Iraq. The brief rainy season is over in the desert here and now the heat builds along with the ever-present sand and dust as summer approaches.

For all practical purposes, it is difficult to distinguish between sand and dust except that one fills every body crevice while the other fills mainly the lungs. Today is one of those days when cooler air holds down the heat that has been broiling soldiers in desert uniforms and equipment. The downside is that the wind seems to come as well, kicking up voluminous clouds of Kuwaiti dust.

If you can imagine a fine, misty dawn in the mountains or a fog in the heavy humidity of a midwest summer morning — the kind where you can hardly see fifty feet in front of you — then just substitute that fog for whitish dust with a reddish, tan tinge, and you can understand the dust storms that soldiers encounter here.

The chapel tent of Camp Virginia is somewhat of an oasis from the billowing clouds of airborne particles. Somewhat is the key word here. The tent is a help, but eventually is so porous to the dust that a mini-fog envelopes the inside of the tent and it is most decidedly not the cloud of God's presence that the Israelites saw in the Tabernacle in the wilderness!

Any self-respecting altar guild would, of course, be in an uproar if this much dust inhabited the sanctuaries of our churches back home, and rightly so. Unfortunately, the ladies of the Altar Guild are not high on the Army's list of deployed mission essential troops, so the dust piles up daily everywhere and on everything despite the best efforts of the chaplain assistants. As I wrote on a tablet in a similar dust storm a few days ago, I was literally compelled to wipe off the tablet with my hand every few minutes. Write, wipe; write, wipe; write, wipe became the mantra like a windshield wiper in a rainstorm.

It was then that a temptation common to all parish pastors struck. I began to muse how I could get a sermon illustration out of this pervasive dust.

Of course, being a pastor always on the prowl for a good story or illustration for the next sermon, I gave in to temptation and thought that dust like this could be compared to God's love and grace. The Lord, too, is everywhere and pervasive and has a seemingly never-ending supply of love for his dusty humanity.

But today in another dust storm, it occurs to me that dust is not the best way to illustrate God's presence and love. Dust is not welcomed by most of us. It makes us choke, hack, cough, and fill our nice red bandanas with sinus matter. It is no fun to sleep in. It is no fun to constantly need to clean out your nose and even ears from its grittiness. Nor is dust pleasant to the taste. I discovered the hard way what common sense would naturally dictate. One should never take an ice cream cone out of the chow tent in a dust storm to eat on the way back to the chapel. The cone is like a magnet for swirling sand, although it does provide a never-ending coating to lick off.

Yes, desert dust is everywhere, but no, it will not do to describe an awesome God of love and power. As a description of sin and its consequences, dust fits very well, but not as a metaphor of life and love.

Dust as sin, dust as death, fits all too well. It is everywhere, in everyone, and on everything. It is as pervasive as disease is among humanity, a dusty disease that causes all to die, that brings pastors to pronounce "earth to earth, ashes to ashes, dust to dust" in cemeteries day after day until the day comes when it is the turn of some younger pastor to do the same over the pastor's mortal remains.

This disease of epidemic proportions inhabits not just individuals, but institutions like the Army, the church, and even our homes, because that is where people live and work. It is in our thoughts, words, and deeds — even in our very best thoughts, words, and deeds. It cannot be escaped, or evaded. It can be denied perhaps, but never escaped. It is genetic, passed on from human parents to human children. Whether we blame it on Adam or not, the fact is that we all have fallen from God's presence. We are separated from our loving Creator. We bear the awful consequences of such sinfulness (Romans 3:23; 6:23). Because of that, we, created from dust are now doomed to return to that same dust in death through war, disease, or even old age.

> *For the wages of sin is death, [wrote Paul. Earth to earth, ashes to ashes, dust to dust] but the free gift of God is eternal life in Christ Jesus our Lord.*
> — Romans 6:23 (NRSV)

Sure dusty sin and death are everywhere, but when God sends his Son to forever break its chains of slavery over our souls, his sacrificial love surpasses even the pervasiveness of sin and death.

> *... but where sin increased, grace abounded all the more.* — Romans 5:20 (NRSV)

What we could not do for ourselves against the storms of sin and the dusty clouds of despair, pain, and suffering that keep us miserable and separated from God, Jesus Christ comes and does for us. He disperses the clouds of sin and death by his death and resurrection and purifies our dusty souls so that we are fit for his purposes now and his kingdom, beyond death forever.

"Dust to dust" pretty much describes the life of a soldier in Kuwait and Iraq. All the troops understand dust's ability to infiltrate and contaminate everything, and every part, of the body. They also are aware of its deadly consequences. This is a time of war and many have been close to its devastation. A soldier understands death better than many in the civilian world, because here they are not sheltered from it. Here its potential to cut down the young, promising lives in an ancient and dangerous profession of arms is out in the open and not hidden away in hospitals, funeral homes, or in the evading of dusty death through flights into entertainment and death.

Soldiers come to the chapel and to chaplains all over camps and assembly areas in this dusty place, well aware that this dust may settle on them, striking them in an instant. They come for answers.

As a Christian, I can give them only one answer. I cannot promise them that they will return from the mission, that the SCUD will never make it to the ground, that the bullet will miraculously strike the Bible in their pocket and save their lives. I have no magic potions, no amulets offering protection, no crosses on their dog tags guaranteed to repel 7.63 rounds from an AK-47 awaiting in ambush.

I can only give them this: The God whose powerful love has broken the chains of death's dusty grip in Jesus the Risen Savior is here. Entrust yourself to him, and he will bring you safely home to his kingdom.

This is what chaplains have to offer. Chaplains offer the promise of God, no better and no worse than the same one offered to those on the brink of death in a hospital intensive care room or at the baptism of a child or an adult or to a grieving family. It is God's pervading grace, his gift of forgiveness and a new life to all bold enough to receive it.

It seems too inadequate, such a small entity, so seemingly helpless a thing in the midst of the sandstorms of life raging all around. In a technical and materialistic society, this message seems utterly vague, and so mysterious. But it is what God has given us in the midst of dusty sin and death. It is what materialistic culture can never offer.

We hear the distant echo of the ancient victory shout, "He is risen!" and 2,000 years later, dusty hearts and liberated souls even through grieving tears shout back, "He is risen, indeed!" and the tiny, seemingly pitiful answer of God brings peace — a quiet confidence, an assurance that no price tag, no thing, can offer.

Somehow, in the miracle of God's power, this message so quiet, so seemingly small amidst the thunderous booms, explosions, and blasts of life and war does its work. Somehow, God's message of love and life clears out sin's heavy layers of fear and alienation and new hearts emerge with a strong confidence and trust in the one who couldn't be held in the grave. I can understand dust, but such powerful, redeeming cleansing love? I don't understand how God does it, but these simple, powerful words spoken so softly to so few women at the tomb on that first Easter morning, somehow they change the hearts of soldier after soldier even millennia later.

How can any of us understand the power of God in wiping away dusty death's residue in our lives both here and for all eternity? Maybe we don't need to understand it. All we need to know is that the same loving Lord who transforms young soldiers when they hear those words so inadequately spoken by the chaplain or anyone else, will do the same for all who put their lives in the hands of the Savior.

In doing so, in this mystery of faith, we are all strengthened for what lies ahead, whether in combat, in the operating room, or wherever we find ourselves in peril and danger, knowing that in life and death we belong to Christ and that we will never be alone again.

If dust — tons of dust — can bring us to our senses, to our knees, to the cross and empty tomb of our Lord, then maybe dust isn't such a bad thing, after all.

So, on a dusty morning when we shake out the sand from our sleeping bags, plowing out our ears and shoveling out the tent for the umpteenth time as we choke on what seems like the dust of the whole land mass of the Arabian Peninsula, we can confess with confidence, even when the dust coats our ice cream, or we hear the chaplain or pastor read from the funeral committal service, "Earth to earth, ashes to ashes, dust to dust." Then we can say confidently, "Go ahead dust. Do your worst in war or in peace. My Lord has already won the victory for me."

"Christ is risen!" Three little, but mighty, words ring in transformed souls and forever change the dreaded presence and meaning of *dust* in our lives.

Dust to Dust? No! Dust to Life!

Thanks be to God who has won the victory through our Lord Jesus Christ. Christ is risen, indeed! Alleluia!

Stolen Altar

"Someone stole your altar, Chaplain?"

This became the familiar question for a week or more after it happened.

The table with a nicely engraved sign "In Remembrance of Me" simply disappeared from the tent that served as the chapel at Camp Virginia in the Kuwaiti desert.

Like Jimmy Hoffa or Amelia Earhart, it just disappeared. This is not an easy thing to do when you are in a tightly controlled military camp preparing for war. It is not easy, either, to flabbergast or stump soldiers. Most have seen, and heard, just about everything in this man's Army, but this one even befuddled the hardest bitten skeptics in desert camouflage uniforms for whom there is nothing new under the sun, or little that could yet amaze them.

One officer, a major, when I earlier kidded him about not being at Mass (I don't know if he was a Catholic or not, but with a very Irish name like O'Malley, what would you guess?) laughed, said he knew he was going straight to hotter places than Kuwait, waved his hand through his close-cropped reddish hair and shook his head asking, "Did someone really steal your altar, Chaplain?"

"Yep."

He, again shook his head in disbelief. He mistakenly had thought that he had seen and heard it all already in his Army career.

This pilfering took place a week or so before the war in Iraq began, and while many soldiers who were dumbfounded by this turn of events wouldn't themselves be caught anywhere near the chapel (unless the SCUD bunkers were all full during an alert and there was nowhere else to go), every soldier still has this innate sense that there are certain things in life, particularly on the eve of combat, that are not very smart to do — like messing with the "Man Upstairs" and his stuff.

The missing altar was even more astounding to these troops. In combat zones, even the most unbelieving of soldiers sense a need to cover all their bases or at the very least to not provoke any divinity that may be paying attention to anger. This superstition, and one that you are somehow a little safer with the chaplain on your side in the SCUD bunker is erroneous, but yet very useful, was not discouraged by most chaplains.

More often than not, sitting in the bunker one can hear even through the muffle of protective masks, a nervous "Well, at least we have a chaplain in here with us. We're safe." The chaplain, thinking for once that silence is the best response, is usually muttering, "I don't feel safer, but what they don't know won't hurt them."

So the disappearance of the altar flew in the face of all accepted soldierly intuition and logic. As the days progressed the question morphed to "Did you get your altar back, Chaplain?" to which the normal response was "Nope, not yet."

We never did.

It was gone like a piece of paper in a Kuwaiti sandstorm. The funny thing was — I, as the chapel coordinator, couldn't even get angry about it. As indignant as I tried to be, I always ended up shaking my head and then laughing about it. It was too incredible, too improbable, too weird, to even get upset about it.

The solution to our missing piece of important chapel furniture?

My chaplain's assistant and I dug two shipping crates out of the dumpsters only fifty yards from the chapel entrance. A sergeant saw us inside the dumpster lifting and shoving the crates out and asked what we were doing. I said we were making an altar. He merely looked quizzical and like many, walked away puzzled. I suppose the chaplain superstition died for him that day. Oh, well.

But we found that these two crates, when stacked one upon the other and nailed together, were just the right height and size to serve as an altar for our worship of God, whose presence graces us even in the arid wilderness. Two plastic liter water bottles filled with sand and covered by tin foil then formed our finely crafted, delicate, field-expedient vases for the plastic roses that never needed watering and graces our new, rugged altar, an altar I discovered that I liked far better than the previous, more finely crafted one.

The former altar was nicely done by field military standards and more of a Bible camp, church camp type, with a rustic flavor. But our new shipping crate altar was more crude and rough, unpainted, unaltered and just as plain as wood made for rough handling and common purposes can be. It was full of nail holes; mostly nail holes from an abundant effort to prevent it from succumbing to the rigors of being shipped overseas. It had plenty of dings and divots from that long journey to the desert.

I was sitting in worship one Sunday morning preparing my mind to preach the sermon and in my meditation began to stare at our crude altar. It was then that it dawned on me that this rectangular symbol of God's presence reminded me more of Jesus than so many fancy, polished, and beautiful altars I had seen over the years in ornate sanctuaries. Was Jesus' cross beautiful, polished, or perfectly hewn and sanded? Or was his cross full of nail holes as well? Surely he was not the first and only Jewish man in Jerusalem to be put to death with that same wooden Roman instrument of death?

Then wouldn't Jesus understand what it meant to be ordinary in so many ways as a human being, despite being God clothed in human flesh? Yes, Jesus was as common as I am, as most of us are, in a world that worships the high and mighty and fancy, but rarely celebrates the ordinary.

Jesus knew what it meant to walk in dust and live in its permeating presence just like this rough altar sitting in the dust and sand that fills the floor, continually covering the exquisite tin foil vases holding plastic roses every time a strong wind blows from any direction.

This is an altar so much more like me, the real me as a believer in the crucified and risen Christ, than any other I have presided, worshiped, or stood before. I am one who yearns to be exquisite and finely crafted, but who struggles to muster even the faith of a small mustard seed. I am dinged up and gouged by life, by failure, inadequacy, and little faith, and am covered by sin and death's dust. I know deeply that I need a Savior who is not repelled by what he sees — this common, ordinary, unremarkable child of God.

That's why this pockmarked and nail-scarred altar is so special to me. It reminds me again of a nail-scarred Savior who loves ordinary, little, unremarkable people in the desert, in farm fields, in office cubicles in cities, or wherever those who call upon the name of Jesus find themselves. People dignified, forgiven, and made important to God through faith in an ordinary man of Nazareth and also a remarkable Savior hanging on a crude wooden contraption of wood in an ancient Jerusalem garbage dump.

So, the chaplain is still not upset by the missing altar, puzzled some perhaps, but not upset. This theft reminded me again that our God does not dwell in the high and fancy sanctuaries of the world, but in the ordinary, humble human heart wherever it finds itself rejoicing in the mercy and wonder of an awesome God who delights to enter into seemingly insignificant hearts of people like you and me.

Whether on the tailgate of a Hummer, or in a dusty tent in the wilderness, God's presence is never shut out or curtailed by the furniture of our worship setting. They merely serve as a place to focus hearts and faith on the God who loved us so exquisitely that he would eat dust, experience loss, pain, betrayal, and death so that we could live in hope, joy, and life.

And if you happen to see an altar with "In Remembrance of Me" on it, looking like it might have been in the desert of Kuwait, tell the owners to just keep it. We have another altar that we like even better and it, by the way, is solidly nailed down to the chapel floor, and in our hearts.

P.S. Please don't tell the troops that their superstition about taking care of the chaplain is a bunch of baloney. We get a lot of favors that we'd just as soon not live without out here in the desert of Kuwait.

Cain And Abel

"Cain" was printed on his nametag in crisp brown lettering that would grab the attention of most chaplains. Military uniforms, especially the desert camouflage uniforms of the Army in Kuwait and Iraq, show up the rank and name of the soldier well compared to the more subdued tones of the green battle dress uniforms of the United States or Europe.

Name and rank are the two things a soldier gets used to looking for when encountering another soldier for the first time.

His biblical name jumped right out at me as he walked through the low tent flap into the yellow interior of the tent we use as a chapel in Camp Virginia. Thousands of soldiers come through this camp and others, primarily getting prepared to go into Iraq or to return here for supplies before heading back into the war.

He was a young specialist, or to those unfamiliar with the military rank structure, someone near the bottom of the Army food chain. He is a step below sergeant and therefore by definition a worker bee in the Army's way of operating.

I was sitting in my usual spot to one side of the long tent used as a chapel reading a military newspaper, *The Stars and Stripes* which was a mere two weeks old. The headlines proclaimed, "War with Iraq Near" which was, of course, old news. Our troops were then already approaching Baghdad and the little news we heard said that an ominous battle loomed.

Specialist Cain grabbed a chair as I motioned him over and asked what I could do for him. His question took me aback. "Sir, I need someone to tell me about Christianity." Even in a war zone, not many soldiers are that direct about religion as they talk to chaplains, most of whom wear the brown cross of a Christian chaplain on their collar.

"Well, I think I can help you, but first tell me what you know about the Christian faith," I asked.

He confided that he did not know much. His parents had left the church early in his life due to the all-too-familiar church fight. He had had no real connection with the faith, so he knew very

33

little. Continuing, he explained why this inquiry was so important to him.

"I've been up in Iraq since the war started and we are going back in a day or two. I just felt like I needed to know more before I went back up there."

His eyes and his body language suggested that he had been in combat and seen far more than he had ever imagined for a young man in his twenties. There was no panic or desperation in his voice, but the deep concern of a young man who has had to grow up quickly in the fear, confusion, and struggle for survival in combat.

"What's Christianity about, Sir? I need to know."

"It's a rescue mission: God's POW raid deep into enemy territory. The difference is that it's God doing the rescuing, not a special operations team."

Military analogies come easily to people who live, eat, and breathe soldiering 24 hours a day, seven days a week, for months at a time. There are no breaks, no days off in war. It is just military all the time.

"From the first book of the Bible," I continued, "to the very last is the story of God's stubborn love for us; how God wouldn't give up going as far as sending his own Son to die for us to bring us back into God's family. Christianity is more of a relationship with a loving God than a system of doctrine or principles."

He pondered. I continued.

"The best thing about God's love is that it is free. We call it grace. No one can earn it or be good enough for it. It can be received from God through Jesus only as a gift."

We talked more about the faith as soldiers shuffled in and out of the tent looking for devotional material or Bibles or even a piece of free candy from the plastic bucket formerly known as a yogurt container. I could not help but sense that the soldier's first question, of all the subsequent ones, was the real question on his mind. It was also easy to connect his name, Cain, to the biblical story and the story of every soldier in every war of human existence.

The first murder recorded in the Bible came as human anger arose in the first Cain. His jealousy at the better sacrifice of his brother, Abel, began the tragic history of brother killing brother.

The curse of Cain was called a mark, but perhaps it can also be seen as the curse of war. God goes to war, as well, against this power, this curse, that brings death and pain. His raid to free hostages from sin and death's iron grip has succeeded in Jesus' death and resurrection.

The young descendant of Cain sat, head down, quietly thinking. It was time for the chaplain to shut up and let God's Spirit do God's work in silence.

"Sir," he said, "I'd like to think some more about this, but if I want to receive this gift can I come back tomorrow and do that and be baptized before I go back to Iraq again?"

"I'll be here all day. I'd be happy to do that."

He left the tent and I have never seen him again.

I can only speculate, of course. Perhaps his unit moved back sooner than expected. Perhaps he decided that the gift was not for him — this relationship with God. Perhaps ... perhaps ...

Now, I find myself hoping that there are nametags in heaven. Not necessarily those of the U.S. Army, but just something that will enable me to one day recognize a name like "Cain" written on those heavenly robes.

Oh sure, the first, biblical Cain will be fine. But the Cain I am hoping to see is the one I knew in Kuwait on his way back to the battlefield, who in his own way, and in his own timing, received the gift of Jesus Christ, the risen Abel, the risen Savior.

That's the Cain and Abel I want to see. The Cain who found life everlasting in the desert of Kuwait in a war in the ancient land of Iraq where the first Cain lived so long ago.

This time, Cain, the American Cain found the gift of life, forgiveness, and eternal life in the Christ, Jesus the Savior, our Lord.

A Can Of Folgers

It's amazing what a can of Folgers coffee can do.

Oh, sure, for us old soldiers (anyone over thirty is "old" in the Army today) who were raised on strong, almost brutal coffee as young officers and NCOs, there is the joy of tasting its fortitude early in an Army morning. But, the camp chapel here in the desert of Kuwait has no fellowship hall and no such coffee brewing. Our morning taste of Folgers is short lived. It is found only in the mess hall (for some reason the U.S. Army insists on eradicating the venerable term "mess hall" in favor of the bland DFAC (dining facility). But the fact of the matter is that mess seems far more appropriate most of the time.

Folgers cans still have a life in the Army after the grounds are gone. Usually they end up being "butt cans" for the far too many young soldiers who still smoke in this day and age. Thankfully, smokers, even in the Kuwaiti desert, must exit the tents to designated smoking areas and thus the need for a "butt can" arises. (The sand for the can is free and readily available everywhere.)

The chapel uses these cans as well, but not for the remains of cigarettes. Ours has a plastic lid on it with a slot cut in the middle and a hand-printed sign taped to its side that instructs, "Prayer Requests." A pad lies next to this emptied coffee can that instructs, "For Prayer Requests Only," followed by more words that remind all readers that it is a violation of the Ten Commandments to run off with the chaplain's pen. (GIs are notorious pen thieves, second only to parish pastors.) Most soldiers reason that the chaplain won't mind or surely the chaplain would forgive such an infraction. They really need a pen. The chaplain is a nice person ... blah, blah, blah.

Well, the chaplain does mind because he is running out of pens! There isn't a bank or funeral home on every corner in the desert here to get free pens like from back home, don't you know?

On the spur of the moment one day, I found the can. Putting a sign on it that rechristened it as a prayer request receptacle, I doubted that rough, tough soldiers would take the time to write out anything. (Maybe to get a free pen, but not a prayer petition!) But, I discovered otherwise.

Soldiers in desert camouflage and full battle rattle, as the troops call all their weighty field and chemical gear, shuffle in and out of the chapel all day. It is on the way to the mess hall (tents). Sometimes they come in to talk, or to look for Bibles because they have lost theirs elsewhere or, occasionally, they seek temporary shelter from the biting wind bearing the airborne sand which stings at all exposed skin.

They take the Bibles, rosaries, and devotionals and some glance at the coffee can, pause, and then stoop over in their Kevlar helmets and slung weapons, take the pen, write a prayer request and drop it in the slot. Often after a "Thanks, Sir," they stoop to exit through the low tent flap and head down the concertina wire-lined dirt and sandy paths of Camp Virginia propelling a "puff" of dust with each step of their desert boots.

As the camp pastor and as a mobilized Army Reserve chaplain, I later gather these requests to pray myself and to make sure that other chaplains have access to them for corporate times of worship. As I sift through them, I am amazed at the selflessness of the petitions. We older ones lament the self-centeredness of so many young people of America who care, we are told, only for their own pleasure and satisfaction.

These requests do not bear that notion out. Here are young Americans far from home in a combat zone. Some are not very close to danger, other than the occasional SCUD aimed at us in the rear areas, but the overwhelming concerns found within the Folgers prayer can are not for themselves. Surprisingly, the prayer requests are for those struggling and in danger and in pain back home. I am astonished as I read through them:

- The mom who recently lost her father in death and a son lost in prison and now a son somewhere in Kuwait and places unknown, for her to be strengthened;
- The agonizing prayer of a soldier thousands of miles away from his wife and young son, that his wife's heart might be softened to give their dying relationship another chance;
- The soldier's friend terminally ill with five brain tumors and awaiting her time to be ushered into the presence of God;
- A son with a growth on his leg and in need of surgery;

- A general prayer for safety for their spouses and children back home.

These are not the prayers of narcissistic youth and hard, uncaring soldiers that Hollywood depicts. These are soldiers far from home who are discovering that their safety is a concern far down the list of worries worthy to be laid before their God. Their safety in battle is nothing compared to the well-being of those they love and care for.

There are many prayers for their comrades, too.

- For my fellow soldiers fighting;
- For teams back from a mission and for those going out on a mission, that they be protected and strengthened;
- A generic prayer for a "whole battalion."

There is also the prayer request that sounds much like one our Lord prayed as he struggled for strength in his own battle in Gethsemane. A soldier writes, "Pray for my strength in the Lord. I want to do everything in his will for me to do."

There are the sad requests for "the fallen" and their loved ones. Clearly this is just not another exercise or training mission and they know it. This is real war, with real casualties, and not in some anonymous place on television halfway around the world.

The realization in minds and souls of these new American warriors is that the latest casualty may have been a soldier who shared a joke with them in the long chow line, or who taught them new and unique ways to curse the Army system while waiting for another anthrax shot. The latest one who fell may have huffed and puffed next to them, donning a gas mask inside the SCUD bunker after the latest siren, or who after the long wait for a free fifteen-minute phone call, shared his joy at hearing his daughter call him "Daddy," despite being deployed in far away lands for three-quarters of her young life.

The price of freedom — theirs, ours, and others — dawns on them and they pray — not for themselves, but for those back home.

Gently, I knock the omnipresent and thickening dust off these amazing requests and after the final one, I silently intone, "Lord, hear our prayer." Automatically my thoughts flow into words I have spoken hundreds and hundreds of times at the altar in my civilian parishes and in ministry, "Into your hands, O Lord, we commend all for whom we pray, trusting in your mercy, through Jesus Christ our Lord. Amen."

Trusting in your mercy. Yes, Lord, trusting in *your mercies*. Again, gently I replace these holy petitions of fellow soldiers half my age back into the red Folgers can on a dusty, crudely constructed table more reminiscent of an old table in the back shed than for a chapel in the United States Army. I think that these young troops really ought not say "Thank you, Sir" to me ever again; for it is I who ought to say "Thank you" to them. I stand in awe of the selfless spirits and praying hearts.

Glancing one last time at their requests, the words of Saint Paul come into focus through my increasingly sand-scratched bifocals. Imprinted on my notepad, they contain the words of Philippians 4:13 (NRSV): "I can do all things through him who strengthens me."

I know that the God who created these soldiers to know his love will be with them wherever this "Operation" takes them, that this loving God will answer their selfless petitions for the sake of the one who also was selfless for the sake of others, for me, for you, and for a lost and perishing humanity, the same Jesus Christ, the crucified and risen Savior to whom the prayer requests are directed with such faith and confidence.

Like I said, it's amazing what a red can of Folgers coffee can do, especially when the coffee is long gone.

Battle Rattle

Leaning low and pulling aside the tent flap, he entered, his SAW [squad automatic weapon] leading the way at his side just like dozens of soldiers do daily when they enter this place of worship in the Kuwaiti desert.

In full battle rattle (all the combat equipment soldiers carry into battle), the young soldier stood by the entrance of the chapel tent unsure of what to do next. Motioning to my chaplain's assistant to go and ask if we could help him, the young assistant escorts him to the dusty table where I sit and says: "Sir, he wants to talk with a chaplain."

He is young, only a private first class, in the Army less than two years. He wears the patch of a special recon unit whose job is to watch the enemy deep in their own territory and return to report about it.

Spreading the legs of his weapon's bipod, he puts it down beside us, looking very thoughtful and pensive. "Sir, tomorrow I'm going on a mission and I wondered if you'd pray for me? I'm a little nervous and I want to make sure I'm right with God before I go."

This has been a common request of chaplains during these days of war in Iraq. We talk as I seek to learn more of his background and faith.

"My mom is a Catholic and my dad a Protestant," he says, "so I spent all day Sunday in church." He explains that he has been a Christian for a long time. He's had his ups and downs, "but I know I belong to God."

"So you are nervous about this mission?" I ask.

"Yes, Sir. A little. But I'm not afraid of dying. I know I would be safe with Jesus. I'm nervous for the guys I'm going with. They have wives and kids. I don't even have a girlfriend — I'm the machine gunner and in a firefight, it may be my weapon that determines whether they live or die."

Trying to put on my best counseling face, but becoming very intrigued by this young man, I discover that like most young soldiers he is not a cold-blooded killer ala Rambo or super-action

41

hero, but a young man concerned that he might have to kill others who like himself are just doing their job, doing what they are told, the enemy who also have families, go to birthday parties, or cheer their favorite sports teams as do American soldiers.

"PFC, I've never been shot at or shot at anyone, but I don't think we can kill another human being in war and not leave a part of our soul behind. Killing is never natural for humans. God didn't create us that way. Yet, sometimes we must kill to protect others. Soldiers fight for principles, but when it all comes down to it, they fight for their buddies beside them — to not let them down or put them in harm's way."

"Yes, Chaplain, and that is what concerns me. I'm afraid that I might let my team down when they need me most. That's what scares me the most."

It is so plain that now even this chaplain can understand. It is not fear of himself dying that brought him to the chapel this night. It is fear of letting down his friends, his comrades, his team. That is not an unusual anxiety among those about to enter harm's way in the military.

The greatest fear they experience is not their own wounding or demise, but of letting down those whose lives depend upon them, letting down those who trust them to do their part.

How different might the church and God's people be if we feared nothing in this world but losing our Savior and letting down God's people and others? If we in the church would rather die ourselves rather than fail to support the needs of our team in the spiritual firefights of this world?

Too often we see the opposite, people scrambling for their own power and prestige, their own agendas, willing to trample on bodies and souls to have their own way rather than to support the squad, the team, the body of Christ in the good fight of faith. Without doubt, not all young soldiers are like this — but this one and many more are.

They are the givers of this world, not just takers and they are what make the Army and the church what it ought to be. They are to the U.S. Army what humble, servant disciples of God's kingdom ought to be to the church.

"Each of you should not look only to your own interests, but also to the interests of others," wrote Saint Paul in Philippians 2.

Here was a young private who understood those words better than so many of his elders, people two or three times his age. I tell him from the depths of my heart that from what I can see, he doesn't need to worry about letting his buddies down. He'll know what to do if, and when, he must. Those, like himself, who are concerned about such things, are always the ones who come through in a pinch. It is the big-mouth braggarts who are the ones to fail more often than not.

We prayed together for his mission, his team, that he might never have to fire his weapon in anger or in battle, and we prayed for a safe, quick return. I tell him to come by and tell me how things went when he returns and then I grab his hand with both of mine for a parting handshake, borne more of respect and admiration than polite courtesy. He leaves the chapel quickly with a lighter step than when he entered even with all his normal battle rattle clinging to his body and the heavy SAW (machine gun). He waves and smiles before ducking through the tent flap into the desert night simply saying, "Thanks, Chaplain."

Settling down again to my dusty chair and table, I cannot help but think, "No, he will never let his buddies down. His team can always depend on him. He will be more than adequate."

"Lord," I then pray, "may the same be said of me in whatever mission you call me." I then pray again, "And Lord? May that be true for your church as well, as we step lightly with a smile into our own night, having learned this vital lesson of not letting our Lord or buddies down."

It is a critical reminder to God's people from Jesus and a young private first class in full battle rattle.

R.H.I.P. Servants

"A waste of a good infantry officer," the lieutenant spoke teasingly while shaking his close-cropped head and walking out of the hot, crowded chow tent. The statement came from a young, hard-charging, Hooah infantry officer and was directed at the old ex-infantryman-turned-chaplain who is more broken-down than hard-charging.

They both shared in common an Army skill badge called the "Expert Infantryman's Badge," that when sewed on the uniform tells other soldiers that here was someone who at least at one time knew the craft of being a ground pounder, an infantryman, well. The fiftyish chaplain (and certainly no longer a hard-charger or an expert infantryman) dared not confess that he had earned his award probably before this lieutenant was born.

What prompted this remark was no great feat of strength, expertise, or daring, but the simple act of greeting soldiers in desert uniforms and pouring them a cup of Army coffee in the morning chow line. The young soldier had observed this routine for several days and was mystified by it. An ex-infantryman, a lieutenant colonel in the United States Army pouring coffee. So undignified, so unworthy of the rank, such a waste. But that hardly seemed the case to the chaplain. I responded to his teasing by saying that this is what happens to broken-down infantrymen when God gets his hands on you and that God now has his number and his turn to take my place was coming.

He smiled as the hot Kuwaiti morning greeted him exiting the tent. Why should such a thing astound him?

It was a simple, but practical thing to do. Soldiers carry a lot of equipment in just the normal course of a day. The Kevlar helmet which cannot, by Army tradition, be worn inside a building (or tent) must be carried along with their weapon and load bearing vest filled with a basic load of ammunition. Throw on the protective mask and ICE pack (individual chemical equipment) and then add a plate of food, cartons of orange juice, and utensils and these soldiers arrive at the coffee machine with no hands left to pour — much less carry — this elixir of Army life, this cup of

45

coffee. Seeing a need, and sensing a chance to greet soldiers, most of whom will never realistically darken the flap of the chapel tent, the broken-down infantryman started offering poured cups to caffeine-needy soldiers. It's too simple and far from earth shattering.

But not for the U.S. Army. This is a rank-conscious institution, which should not come as a surprise to anyone. That also means that R.H.I.P. is very evident. R.H.I.P. means "Rank Has Its Privileges" and one of those privileges is that the higher ranks tend to be served rather than to be serving. Deference goes to each rank above your own as a courtesy, not a right. That's the system, and every soldier from the first week of basic training is taught to understand this.

The reaction to a lieutenant colonel pouring coffee was interesting. Many troops were flabbergasted and didn't know what to say. To try to put them at ease, I attempted to joke with them. "Hey, I'm buying today." "The coffee is on the chaplain corps today. Free refills all day long."

The soldiers get the joke, knowing that Uncle Sam is paying the bill, but the jokes usually do the job and set the troops at ease. They even smile when I say, "This coffee is so strong this morning, it'll put hair on your chest." Male soldiers smile and a few females do as well. Some soldiers reply, "Thanks, Sir, but I need it on my head more" as they show heads devoid of hair that blends in with their high-and-tight field haircuts.

It is not the attempt at humor that confuses them. It is the rankness of the coffee-pouring that breaks the code they have been taught. Most confuse me with someone who is standing in line for a cup and they defer to my rank. "Go ahead, Chaplain. You get your cup first."

"I'm not in line. I'm pouring. Would you like a cup?"

Confusion reigns.

One private, having observed this, like the lieutenant several days before him, could stand it no longer. He came up and asked point-blank, "Sir, why are you doing this?"

I try to explain that it is no big deal. Getting a cup of coffee, unlike a cup of soda at the fountain, is a two-handed operation. You have to have both hands free to charge the cup and soldiers simply don't have two free hands. So I thought I could help and also greet the soldiers here. But the real reason is more biblical. Didn't Jesus say, "For the Son of Man came not to be served, but to serve"? (Mark 10:45 NRSV).

R.H.I.P. does not compute in God's scheme of things. Jesus said, "No," to that rank-conscious thinking and lifestyle. The disciples, we find, were just as clueless to this "inverse" spiritual economy as anyone today. The night before Jesus' own death after the Lord's Supper, those closest to Jesus began to argue who would be the greatest in the coming kingdom. Presumably, that meant, "Who gets to serve me?" instead of, "Who do I get to serve?"

But Jesus countered that we are not to be like that. "Instead, the greatest among you should be like the youngest [lowest?] and the one who rules [commands?] like the one who serves" (Luke 22:26 NRSV).

Serving is no complex matter for theologians in ivory towers. Most service is simple, filling needs, often unasked and unnoticed by others. Whether in the church or in the military, simple acts of service are just following in the footsteps of the Master, who humbly served by washing the disciples' feet and who gave his life in humble service. This is what matters to God — service, not privilege. Servants are what our Lord calls us to be in a rank-conscious world, employing a type of humble, simple service that befuddles this world where R.H.I.P. reigns.

So, the next time the pastor is invited to be the first in line at the congregational potluck, don't be surprised if he says, "No thanks. I'd rather pour coffee for those who need an extra hand." And when he does that, please, no one say, "A waste of a fine pastor."

Before you begin to think what a fine, wonderful servant the ex-infantry chaplain is, please know I've never offered to wash the chow hall dishes for the KPs (kitchen police).

After all "R.H.I.P."

Service is never a waste of a Christian — chaplain or otherwise.

I Ain't Never Seen A Porta-Pottie I Couldn't Lick, But I Had Some Close Calls

Now before your imagination goes too far with the title, "lick" in this sense means "to whip, to defeat, to whoop up upon" as in a battle, fight, or brawl.

Metaphors, particularly mixed metaphors, can be rather dangerous. The "Sustainer Inn" back in Wiesbaden, Germany, contained one such mixed metaphor. A computer-generated sign adorned each stall in the latrine back in "the land of flush toilets." It contained a clip art picture of a birthday cake complete with a candle and the words "It's a piece of cake to keep the restroom clean. Clean up after yourself."

Now, I understand perfectly the intent of the message, but somehow "cake" and "restroom" just don't produce the best image in most people's minds, just like the image of "licking a porta-pottie" unless it means to "overcome, conquer, or defeat."

The problem here is twofold.

First is that porta-potties are the modern equivalent of a field latrine. With thousands of troops in one area here at Camp Virginia, just digging holes in the ground wherever one feels like it just won't do. Imagine the poor individual being awakened in the middle of the night for a SCUD alert and finding the nearest hole in the ground to flop their body down only to discover that someone else has made it a latrine first.

No, that just wouldn't do in the U.S. Army!

Another challenge with the porta-potties out in the desert is that the wind can blow awfully hard and if you've ever found yourself freshening up in a porta-john in such a strong wind, it can be a rather moving experience.

Perhaps most have seen the commercial of the comedian who is at an outdoor concert with his girlfriend when she uses a porta-pottie. While he is jiving to the music a bit too enthusiastically, he bumps the port-pottie over the side of the embankment while the viewer's imagination provides the "juicy" details. It is a pretty funny commercial — that is, until you find yourself swaying inside one such device in a sandstorm.

The porta-potties have a securing rope over the top to prevent such disasters, but in one such fierce windstorm at Camp Virginia while soldiers were battling to keep their tents up, more than one "band of four" porta-potties "bit the dust" face down. Thankfully, no one was inside when they tumbled down like the walls of Jericho, but there could hardly be a worse way to earn a Purple Heart for being wounded in action. "Gee, Grandpa, how did you get your Purple Heart in the second Gulf War?"

"Well, sonny, there was this porta-pottie in a windstorm one dark night and...."

All kidding aside, there would be absolutely no way out of a porta-pottie that fell over on its door. A person would simply be trapped until rescued by someone the next morning. I shudder to think of such a fate.

The second problem is the possessiveness of those plastic outhouses. This is the issue that is the most common.

Because of all the gear soldiers wear, the narrowness of the door can become a genuine engineering challenge. When one dons all the required equipment of web gear, Kevlar helmet, protective mask, and carries a weapon (and in my case a briefcase), it is a royal pain to take it all off and leave it outside the porta-pottie. Plus it is a cardinal sin to leave a weapon, or other sensitive items, unattended (not to mention how difficult it is to chase down a thief with one's pants around one's ankles) so most soldiers prefer to slide into the confines of a facility rather than risk losing their equipment.

Like trouble, however, it is always easier "to get into than to get out of it."

More than once, I found myself getting into the porta-pottie fairly easily, even with all the equipment hanging over me, but discovered that reversing the procedure was nothing short of a struggle.

I could not find the same angle to "disengage from the enemy." And, when skill and intelligence fail to do the trick, there is nothing left but brute force to break away from the clutches of those possessive plastic buildings.

Yanking, pulling, pushing, twisting, turning, grunting, and yelling, all in the effort to free myself, I have no doubt that any other occupants of the other porta-potties would surely have thought that *the poor guy ate too many MREs. That's the worst case of constipation I've ever heard!*

The seconds it took to disengage and to finally pull through the opening into the light seemed like minutes, if not hours, of struggle. It is not a pleasant experience to fear losing a battle to an inanimate object and see your life pass before your eyes in the realization that you are in danger of losing that struggle.

The next time you just stroll into your bathroom at home "in the land of the free" with a *la-de-da* attitude and you don't have to slide in sideways or worry that it might tip over on you and trap you in a strong wind or even fret about how you might possibly be able to exit gracefully with all your equipment and body intact, just pause a moment and say a word of thanks. "Restroom, I have taken you for granted far too long. Thank you, thank you, for being so accommodating to me."

There is many a soldier in the desert who is dreaming this night of home and family and maybe, just maybe of the fair land of flush toilets where the doors are wide and the latrine big enough to read *War and Peace* in comfort.

"I never met a porta-pottie I couldn't lick ... but, lordy, lordy, I had some awfully close calls" in the desert of Kuwait.

A Cookie Dilemma

I faced a terrible dilemma the other day.

Tragically, it is not unusual in a combat zone far from home for deployed soldiers.

Was it life or death? No, but terrible, nonetheless.

A care package had arrived from a loving spouse. It was the first one I received and it was grand and glorious; a box of goodies, including my favorite cookies, baked by my wife; cookies usually only reserved for Christmas back home.

Mouthwatering, savory cookies; a piece of home.

I sat in the dark tent eating some of them a day or two later, trying to stretch out the joy as long as possible.

It was then that I turned on my flashlight to find the next big, delicious morsel and, to my horror, discovered a green, fuzzy mold covering large parts of the remaining cookies.

I suddenly never hated mold this much. How could it do this to these cookies 7,000 miles from home?

It was then that my terrible dilemma ensued. What can one do with cookies so despoiled?

I had to make a horrible decision there in the light of my flashlight.

I made it ...

I turned my flashlight off and finished eating my favorite cookies.

All I Ever Needed To Know, I Learned At The Mess Hall Coffee Urn

This is my favorite place in the whole Army ... the breakfast coffee machine in the dining facility [DFAC] affectionately known to old soldiers as "the mess hall."

"Mess" is the catchier phrase for the chow hall, but to its credit here in Camp Virginia, Kuwait, these facilities perform an amazing feat every day. They feed hot meals to a fluctuating number of soldiers in the thousands who are "inbound" or "outbound" in this Middle Eastern theater of operations. Eight to ten thousand soldiers a day trudge through the sand and dust, laden with all the required gear for an Army to live and fight in a combat zone.

Kevlar (K-Pot vs. the old steel pot) helmet, weapon, load bearing equipment, and a basic load of ammunition of 210 rounds (plus some essential, never-be-without-except-at-your-peril toilet paper), canteens, protective mask and during SCUD threat times an ICE pack (individual chemical equipment).

This is a lot to carry through a chow line where the soldier also receives plastic utensils, napkins, juice, and a plate full of food. The Kevlar helmet suspended from the canteen by its chin strap makes a handy carrying container for extra food items, but no matter how one configures the load, it is too much to carry down crowded aisles crammed with soldiers, chairs, and weapons.

To be a soldier who eats in Kuwait, one must be fairly well-coordinated to get all that equipment and food to a table without spilling or dropping any of it.

As coordinated as they may be, what is really tough is getting a cup of steaming hot coffee while carrying everything else, even as junior mess sergeants yell out "Eat your food and get out! Others need your seat!"

The Army miscalculated badly concerning the number of "hands" it needs to issue to soldiers to carry and handle everything that is offered them. That is where the chaplain gets to have some fun.

55

Sensing an opportunity, I hang out at the coffee urn holding a kazillion gallons of Army "Joe" which can usually double for Humvee motor oil in an emergency or eat holes in Kevlar like battery acid.

Soldiers nearing the end of the chow line glance wistfully at the coffee, make a mental calculation that they cannot possibly pour a cup and still not dump their food over the sand on the chow tent floor, then hear, "Can I pour a cup of coffee for you this morning? It's guaranteed to put hair on your chest — male or female."

They laugh at the chaplain, looking shocked that an officer would pour them coffee, and then usually graciously accept.

It's here that I have met soldiers with interesting names, names like SPC Gump. I couldn't help but ask if he is often called "Forrest."

"All the time, Chaplain!" he says with a weary smile on his face.

"Well, then, I won't call you that again and ruin your breakfast."

Forrest smiles and thanks me.

There was also PFC Love which drew a compliment on his moniker. I hoped his first name wasn't "Strange" and that he wasn't a doctor, but I don't ask. Consuming breakfast is a much greater priority for troops, and justly so.

There was also SGT Church to whom I likewise could not help but make a comment as he walked by. I said that he would make a great chaplain with a name like that. "Chaplain Church" has a real ring to it.

Of course, passing out coffee is more than harassing soldiers about their names.

There were soldiers who asked about services at the chapel. Somehow the word has not gotten out to them or they missed the many signs scattered about.

Other soldiers asked about becoming a chaplain, what it took, how long did it take. Many were dismayed that it took more than being in a Bible study and that seven to eight years of studies beyond high school were required.

Yet another soldier asked about becoming a chaplain assistant as he was not happy in his specialty where violence or force was often expected.

None of these troops had ever talked to a chaplain before about their questions, so seeing a perspiring one at the coffee urn seemed to provide a good non-threatening opportunity to talk.

Planting oneself in the chow hall also gives good HUMINT. That is a great Army term that means "human intelligence." In other words, another human being observes how people are doing rather than a machine or in a report. Exhaustion, loneliness, weariness, apprehension, or jubilation are usually very transparent emotions in the desert.

The passing response to "How's it going this morning?" is usually routine, but sometimes soldiers take the opportunity to say "Bad day, Chaplain. I called home and my wife is not doing so well." Or "My kids are all sick." Or "I really got into it with my platoon sergeant today."

Sometimes it is far easier to unload on a complete stranger whom one will likely not see again than it is to talk to someone who knows you well. A strange chaplain at the coffee urn can be useful beyond the obvious coffee distribution.

You can discover whether troops are moving out or have another stifling day of waiting for their equipment at the port. You find out if their unit is moving north into Iraq and how they are feeling about that.

At the coffee urn one can even meet the "Third Country Nationals" who are working at the chow tent; non-Kuwaitis, usually from Pakistan or India, who have been hired to cook, clean, and serve in the dining facilities. One of the supervisors, Muhammad, was from Pakistan and even worked in Kuwait during the Iraqi invasion of 1990. He told his story of surviving that ordeal and getting back home. He had two sons in the university in Pakistan and this was the best way he could support them. Talking with Muhammad was a treat at the coffee urn.

Every pastor must find the place where ministry can be done, a place where the good news is taken to the people rather than expecting the people to come to it. Fewer and fewer people are coming to the church so it is a no brainer that the church should go where the people live, work, and even eat. I believe that is what

Jesus did, did he not? Of course, Jesus got into trouble doing that precise thing.

But exactly when did Christians begin to believe that the world ought to stomp, slide, or drag itself to the pastor or into our sanctuaries in order to have a personal, human connection with the Lord? Ninety-five percent of the time "It ain't gonna happen."

But what if Christians planted themselves where the people walk, talk, eat breakfast, drink coffee, or even play cards? What could we learn about their lives, hopes, dashed dreams, fears, and joys by walking on their turf and even in their shoes (desert boots)?

It probably is a big overstatement to say that "everything" I learned about the gospel and ministry, I learned at the coffee urn, but if the truth be told, I've learned a lot about Forrest Gump, SPC Love, and lots of other soldiers in the desert just by filling up cups of coffee in the chow tent.

I wonder where God can plant you as a follower of Christ and turn simple, everyday needs into opportunities to serve others in the name of the Savior, Jesus?

Flowers In The Desert

The last of the big rains came to the Kuwaiti desert. "No more until November," they said.

So when it came, it exposed some holes in the chapel tent here at Camp Virginia. Besides the leaky holes in the tent roof, the water also flowed down the sides of the large fest tent and onto the plywood floors creating mini-"streams in the desert" as the prophet Isaiah wrote.

One strategic leak was over the altar at the west end of the chapel. The altar consisted of two wooden packing crates nailed together and recently rescued from the dump.

Two vases of flowers perched precariously on the altar, often prone to falling over in strong gusts of wind. As the rain came and the leak started to flow, it seemed that a miracle was taking place.

The leak was perfectly situated to drop precisely into one of the flower vases on the altar. God was watering the flowers in his house in this desert with life-giving, rare moisture.

Dead center was the dripping flood of water.

But I couldn't help but wonder if God knew that the flowers were ... artificial?

Who said God doesn't have a sense of humor?

A Life Well Spent

*... if you want to end your days in the golden afterglow
of life well spent ...*

Those words rose up and grabbed me like few others have of
late.

... life well spent ...

They were words written at the end of an introduction to another one of those ubiquitous lists of ten things *everyone* on planet
earth should remember, do, say, keep in mind, live by, and so forth,
found so frequently these days on the internet or in magazines.
Lists at one time we thought were good to remember so we clipped
them out and hung them on the refrigerator door by a free magnet
from some bank or pizza delivery service.

The introduction began:

*If you want to get the greatest happiness out of life, if
you want to lie down every night as a better man or
woman, if you want to continually grow mentally, mor-
ally, and spiritually ...*

Then came the words that caused my eyes to cease scanning
and to stop and think:

*... if you want to end your days in the golden afterglow
of life well spent ...*

Of course! The day will come when most of life will be behind us and we probably pause at some vista in our golden years to
look back reflecting on its meaning, its value, unless that time of
reflection is cut short through a sudden fatal accident or tragedy.

That day of reflection will dawn when we will realize that our
existence on planet earth is more "spent" than has energetic potential remaining; that our lives will be at some point "exhausted,

61

all used up, shot, expended." The tank will be on empty, the low fuel warning light will be flashing, and there will be no refills possible on this side of eternity.

The inevitable question in this realization becomes: "If this is so, if I have no choice in this finite, fragile, human existence but to accept that it will end, how, then will I spend this life and for what purpose so that one day I can end my days in the "golden after-glow of life well spent"?

Most of us would, I believe, desire to finish off our days with greater joy and accomplishment than regret. All who reflect will, of course, see plenty of mistakes, lunacy, and sin in our past, but unless we are morbidly introspective, we will also see how God has used us, wittingly or unwittingly, to love, to do good, to give hope and perhaps even to provide a portion of peace to a miniscule part of this planet.

Yet, the look back that can bring us the golden afterglow by God's grace can probably only take place by our reflecting now, prior to the end, on how we go about spending our lives well.

The question remains: "What does it mean to *spend* our lives and to do it well?"

Spending is not a difficult concept for most of us. We do it all the time, except we normally associate *spending* only with money. We *use* money to provide for our daily needs, purchase our recreation, and to provide solutions for our medical concerns. When we *use* money, we usually say that we *spent* our money so that we exhaust its value by transferring its power to someone else in the form of paper money. Into the cash register goes the bill and it is gone to us. All we have left is the product, the results of the money we spent. In essence, we expend our money.

Currently in the military and in a hostile fire zone, one can't help but think in military terms, especially in the "expending of ammunition." A single round of munitions once fired in propelling a projectile down the barrel of an M-16A2 or a M1 Abrams Tank through explosive gases ignited from a shell is described as "spent ammunition." All of its power, its explosiveness to propel the warhead toward a target is expended, is used up in the firefight, or exhausted.

The remains, the empty shell of the spent ammunition, has little value left except for scrap metal, but the soldier who fired that round can now look to see if it had value by hitting the target. Did the spent round accomplish its mission or was it wasted by missing the target?

That is a "spent" round in the military, the well-spent or poorly-spent life of a single round of ammunition.

But what does a "spent life" of a human being, a "well-spent life" that has hit the target of life look like?

Continuing the round of ammunition metaphor, we see that this piece of explosive power can be used to terrorize, exhort, bully, and intimidate the innocent and helpless, or to kill any who would seek to stop them from being exploited.

A spent round can be used to protect, defend, and liberate those who are oppressed. Police exhibit this quality and one hopes that the military does as well.

Perhaps the saddest case is those rounds of ammunition that are used for nothing in life, that are never expended for good or ill. They just sit content to be unused in any cause, any fight for freedom, human dignity, or justice.

Given a choice (and amazingly God has given all of us a great deal of say in this matter), I would want to end my life "well-spent," having lived a life of meaning in whatever time God allows on this earth, having affected this world or someone in it for good, for God's glory; to somehow make the decisions, the choices, and the opportunities to live in such a way that life, faith, and freedom are brought in greater measure. I want to have lived in such a way that my finite time on earth was used up either explosively in a short, but magnificent burst of faith and good or more likely in a long continuous, steady burn of expending energy that brings more life than death, more protection than harm, more liberty to the body and soul than imprisonment and oppression. I want my life to be expended not just for my own personal gain or comfort, but one that matters for God, for good, and somehow seeks to make a difference, however small and seemingly insignificant, for the Lord's will and to the betterment of my loved ones and neighbors on this earth.

"That was a life well-spent!"

What better benediction and magnificent words could ever be spoken at our funerals or by others at the coffee shop when they hear of our demise, or over any human life at its end?

God has given us the power to choose this as our benediction as we ask ourselves every waking morning, "How will I order my life, my explosive time, and energy this day? What will we spend our life for? For God? For the good of others? Or only for ourselves, our comfort, or our entertainment purposes?"

To "end our lives in the afterglow of a life well-spent."

It is a question not for the old, but for those with gas in the tank of life yet, for the young who have so much living yet to do and for the middle-aged who yet have time and energy to make decisions now that will determine if their life is to be on target or misspent.

Those decisions are ours to make daily, with or without a list of "Ten Things to ..." if we are to hear the words of Jesus as Saint Matthew records.

"Well done, my good and faithful servant...." You have indeed spent your life well! Enter into the afterglow and joy of your Master forever.

"... a life well-spent."

Chain Of Thanksgiving

"Thanks for being here, Chaplain."

"Pardon me?"

"Thanks for being here, Sir. You and the other chaplains. I appreciate all that you do for us. Seeing you here first thing in the morning makes our day. So, thanks, Sir."

It is difficult to catch a chaplain/pastor/teacher at a loss for words. Most parishioners hope and pray that this will happen during the sermon, but it does happen at other times, not often, mind you, but when it does, everyone remembers.

The occasion of this "word holiday" was in a chow line in the desert of Kuwait. It happened with the totally unexpected gratitude of this sergeant in the United States Army.

Hundreds, if not thousands of GIs trudge through one of three large mess tents here in the barrenness of Camp Virginia where the same meal is served every morning varying only in being either a "pancake or French toast" day. (Oh, with the current hard feelings toward the French, I should say "Texas Toast" instead of giving the French any credit.) Otherwise, the same scrambled eggs, sausage, potatoes, SOS, and the occasional grits are precisely the same every day.

This soldier had eaten his Army breakfast and with empty plate and Kevlar helmet in hand plus other essential military field gear hanging all over his body, detoured from the trashcans and exit to where I had stationed myself to greet soldiers and pour coffee. He continued, "I've been up in Iraq, but came back yesterday to go on emergency leave."

Knowing that emergency leaves are generally only granted for the death of immediate family members, I asked if that was the case for him.

Another shock.

"No, Sir. My wife has cancer and has taken a turn for the worse. I need to go home to be with her," he said in a matter-of-fact, soldierly way, but those circumstances are hardly everyday occurrences and obviously this was serious.

"But, Sir, I wanted to just tell you how much I appreciate what you chaplains do. It really helps us. My chaplain up north (in Iraq) helped me a lot. So thanks!"

"God be with you, Sergeant. Have a safe trip home." These pitiful words were all I could dredge up as he departed the tent. I would probably never see him again.

Why was he thanking me? All I was doing was standing around the coffee machine in a tent in the desert. Then the Spirit rapped my dull, Norwegian soul.

"Hey, knucklehead," the Spirit of God whispered, "you're just getting the thanks for the good work others have done in my name. You're reaping the reward of thanksgiving for what I planted, nourished, and watered, using hundreds of other children of God who serve me."

And, of course, the Spirit was right, as always.

We have all been "in the wrong place at the wrong time," usually reaping the reward, the misdeeds others have wrought. But, every once in a while we are "in the right place at the right time," and are the beneficiaries of the praise that others deserve. Others deserved to hear the sergeant's gratitude. The nameless chaplain in Iraq who was there to help deliver the Red Cross message concerning his wife and who most likely smoothed the way for his return home was one of them.

Others were the numerous chaplains who in the past had greeted him, treating him with the dignity of a child of God despite being in a big, oftentimes impersonal Army system. They had, perhaps, shared a cup of coffee with him in the mess hall, or had eaten an MRE on the hood of a Humvee with him or maybe had just eaten dust together on a convoy to and from some strange, but hardly exotic, destination.

The chain continues back in the past. The pastor or priest who encouraged him as a child or rebellious teenager, the Sunday school teacher who week-in and week-out had taught him, and others, of a gracious and loving God who would never abandon him, the parents who modeled, as imperfectly as all parents do, the God who has entered and changed their lives forever, the praise belongs to them, this long chain of faithfulness to the Savior, Jesus Christ.

His words made me recall what is so easily forgotten by Christians in our individual-dominated culture: Ministry is not just for the ordained or those who wear brown crosses sewed on the collars of desert uniforms. It is for hundreds and thousands of individual Christians adding their slice of faithful witness and loving service to whomever God sends into their paths every day.

Each encounter adds a chapter to a glorious book God is writing for each of his children. Each story, each event, fills the soul of the believer so that one day their cup runs over and their hearts overflow with gratitude to God, sloshing and spilling some of that praise on us who don't deserve it a bit.

"I planted. Apollos watered, but God gave the growth," wrote Saint Paul in 1 Corinthians, which we could easily amend to say, "Others planted and others watered, but somehow I got the credit."

This realization doesn't bring pride; rather, it fosters humility and an awed silence at how God works every day in people's lives. It causes me to wonder, too.

Whose link in the chain, whose chapter in life's book, can I add to in the smallest measure today so that in five, ten, or twenty years some other chaplain or pastor or child of God will hear words of gratitude for something in which they had no part at all?

To be perfectly honest, few soldiers consider Kuwait and Iraq to be the "right place and the right time." Those designations are reserved for home, and the sooner the better. But I am one of the few in Camp Virginia, Kuwait, who can honestly say, "I was in the right place at the right time to receive credit that others so richly deserved from a young soldier on his way home to a very ill spouse."

How about you? Have you asked yourself today, "God, I am here in this place and in these circumstances. How can I be of service to you, Lord, to add a word or two to the amazing book you are writing in your people's hearts every single day so that some day, down the road, an unnamed servant of God will have praise and thanksgiving heaped on their undeserving and dumbfounded head because of the faithful witness of little people like me?"

"Thanks, Chaplain, for being here for us!" kept echoing in my soul as I continued to greet soldiers and pour their coffee.

No, the praise isn't mine. It is God's and the humble servants of Jesus Christ who will never be known until we all gather in heaven to sing praise and retell the stories of God's amazing grace book.

The right place at the right time.

Yes, Lord, thank you for this awesome privilege to receive the credit others so richly deserve.

The Spirit's Honeywagon

I doubt too many people sit and meditate on the arrival of a "honeywagon."

Not many, that is, unless they are sitting in a tent in the desert of Kuwait, for one discovers that a person in an Army camp far from home does many things that they would never dream of back in the land of television and flush toilets.

I can't help but look upon this daily occurrence as I sit at my table in the large, yellow fabric, mosque-outline printed interior (a bit of psychological warfare by our Muslim hosts?) that is the chapel of the U.S. Army's Camp Virginia.

In this sprawling tent city that often houses thousands upon thousands of soldiers, airmen, and the occasional Marine and British soldier coming and going from this hostile fire pay zone, there are dozens upon dozens of the modern military's equivalent of a field latrine in every direction. Yes, the pervasive porta-john is everywhere.

Through the chapel's tent flap my gaze weaves through the bamboo poles that keep up "God's house" even in the mighty sandstorms that happen through this camp not far from Kuwait City and the Persian Gulf, I see this daily honeywagon occurrence almost always at the same time. As the Humvees and trucks churn up an already pulverized dust on their way to destinations in Iraq leaving the fine dust to hang in the air to be inhaled by soldiers as they walk by the chapel, a large, green, civilian tanker truck pulls up to the plastic-molded latrines outside the DFAC (aka mess hall, chow tent, botulism palace).

A Middle Eastern civilian (Kuwaiti? Probably not. Big oil money tends to make such professions undesirable for the locals and an opportunity for poorer outsiders) jumps out with a surgical type mask over his nose and mouth accompanied by a soldier in Kevlar helmet, weapon, and full battle gear. (No civilians are allowed unescorted in the camp in this age of terrorism, especially while the hostile war environment continues.)

The honeywagon then does what honeywagons do; they remove the waste and refresh the porta-john for further use.

It is a simple, everyday, and normal thing that is all but hidden from most of the modern western world through our sewage system except, of course, when the pipes break or are clogged up. Then, we pay through the nose, in more than one way, for a plumber to come and fix the problem refilling the hole, leaving us nothing to do but pay the bill and try to grow grass on the spot once again.

Out here there is no such sewage system, leaving only the honeywagons to do their thing.

Field sanitation is one of the less thrilling aspects of an army in the field, but it is essential when you have literally thousands of soldiers confined in the same area. It doesn't make the headlines; no CNN crews have been here to film this daily operation as they did virtually every other military aspect before the Second Gulf War started.

But, ignore sanitation, get lax in cleanliness and hygiene, and the price is very steep in soldiers rapidly becoming disabled through sickness and disease. In the Civil War it is said that more soldiers died from disease that was preventable than from battle losses, and this has been the case in most conflicts throughout history up until the most recent.

I can't say in any of thousands of sermons I've prepared over the years that I have ever thought of comparing the Holy Spirit of God to a honeywagon or a driver of a "sucker," as is one of the more polite names the troops call the wagon. (I pray the Spirit doesn't take offense to this rather uncommon comparison.) But really at its essence, one of the main jobs of the Spirit in a believer's life is very, very similar.

I can't imagine too many congregations would be thrilled to discuss any pastor's porta-john, honeywagon sermon, at least in much detail. This just would not do over coffee, orange juice, and Dunkin' Donuts (if you're lucky enough to get Dunkin' Donuts after church!).

But, soldiers in a deployment are normally reduced to a much more basic level of thinking where niceties are often left for ... well, for people back home eating donuts and drinking coffee back in the land of flush toilets. In all the enforced closeness of living conditions of a camp like this, modesty is usually the first casualty of war.

Yet, within the Christian faith, we have always believed that sin and its consequences are the waste, the byproduct, of our rebellious nature. It is the residue of human life that living Frank Sinatra's song, "I Did It My Way," brings inevitably to all; pain, selfishness, and a downright stench left in its wake.

Even in the best intentioned people, believers and non-believers alike, our lives become examples of brokenness; broken intentions, broken dreams, and broken promises to others and to God, resulting in broken hearts and shattered souls. Whether in small things or the big issues of life, our porta-johns (souls) reek with ill health and disease until they overflow. Something has to be done about this or the diseased soul becomes sicker and sicker until it drowns in its own filth and dies.

The scriptures tell us this is not just some church doctrine dreamed up out of the blue to harass and intimidate poor, weak, and helpless souls. It is, in fact, God's diagnosis (Jeremiah 17:9; Romans 3:23).

But, while God knows the problem, he also knows the solution: The Great Physician. In his mercy God sends his Son to take on all our waste — past, present, and future — hanging on a cross surrounded by the human refuse of ancient Jerusalem's garbage dump. He frees us once and for all from the diseased consequence of our sin and rebellion. On the cross, Jesus breaks the chains that enslave us to this putrid sin and death and cleanses us to become children of God.

Yet even after God works his grace in our lives for that first and glorious time through baptism and the confession of the wonderful name of Jesus, making our relationship with him safe and secure for eternity, the presence of sin, and its harmful waste byproducts, still bedevils our daily lives. The accumulation of "stinking wrongs" in our thoughts, words, and deeds cries out for the Spirit's large, green porta-john truck to make frequent, if not daily, stops in our lives to cleanse us of our burdensome loads of guilt and shame.

Liturgical Christians call this "Confession and Forgiveness," which usually begins normal worship. Ironically, we usually use the "Brief Order for Confession and Forgiveness" when most of

71

our sins require anything *but* brevity. But brief as the list may be, or not, we intentionally invite the Holy Spirit of God to hook up to our souls through the words of 1 John 1:9: "If we confess our sins, he is faithful and just and will forgive our sins and cleanse us from all unrighteousness."

While Jesus has forgiven us once for all time, our own health — mentally, physically, and spiritually — in our relationship with our Heavenly Father requires us to "come clean."

I can almost hear the rumble of the Spirit's truck now as it pulls up daily to my soul; air brakes squawk and hiss as it rolls to a halt and out jumps a shining, pure Spirit. I shouldn't be surprised that he is wearing a strong mask over his face as the stench of my wrongs and failures revolt his purified nostrils.

But, like a loving parent changing a stinking diaper of a baby or wiping up the vomit of a flu-infected child, our loving God cheerfully cleanses the stench from my reeking soul. He even smiles, despite the gruesome, daily, endless task because he recognizes in each of his confessing children the sign of the cross etched on their foreheads through those baptismal waters and the Spirit promises and desires more than anything for us true health and wholeness that can only come from those who make no pretense of hiding their filth from an all-knowing and all-loving God.

Hooking up the suction hose, the Spirit removes quickly, efficiently, and completely every mistake and wrong with malice aforethought in thought, word, and deed and takes it for permanent disposal to the "heavenly waste treatment facility" where it will never, ever be seen or encountered again even on the judgment day.

In its place, the Spirit then pumps pure, cleansing fluids of grace, love, and guidance to restore the soul; refreshing and life-changing fluid that calls us once more to renewal, change, and a joyous sense of service and love for our gracious Savior, our crucified and risen Great Physician.

Each and every day the process is the same for the Spirit and might even be considered boring if that daily grace did not bring us back to a measure of wholeness, encouragement, and peace as God's forgiven people.

The Kuwaiti honeywagon rolls off in a cloud of dust to the next bank of porta-johns and as weird as it may seem, I find myself grateful that I have witnessed this mundane event once again.

Strangely enough, in my gratitude I look forward to its return each day that I find myself in this wilderness in the Arabian peninsula staring out the chapel tent flap; grateful not because it is what most would consider a beautiful sight, but rather because each time I see that "sucker" truck rolling into sight, I am reminded of God's astounding and cleansing Spirit who renews and strengthens me to tackle another day in his love and service.

If you happen to be in a clean, sweet-smelling fellowship hall without tent flaps, standing or sitting with a pretty, flower-patterned Dixie cup of orange juice in your hand or clasping a stout cup of good old coffee with chunks of Dunkin' Donuts stuck between your dentures discussing the grossness of the porta-john illustration in church, here's one more vital thing for you to remember:

Neither the Kuwaiti truck, nor the U.S. Army nor the Holy Spirit provides "t.p."!

Sadly, this is a "B.Y.O.T.P." Army and world.

Eye Contact

"Never make eye contact when the chaplain asks a question, because when you do you're done for!"

Thus teased the Army chaplain as he asked a question of the small group of believers gathered for worship in the dusty tent called Camp Virginia chapel. Trying to make the worship less lecture and more interactive, he would ask these soldiers in their tan and brown desert uniforms a question that led to a thought or point in the sermon. He would ask, and then wait, looking around at various soldiers during the inevitable silence that followed.

Silence.

Finally one of the soldiers commits a tactical blunder. He looks at the clock behind the graying, balding chaplain's head and makes eye contact! It is too late. Now some sort of response must be made and the chaplain teases, with everyone else visibly relieved that they have successfully escaped and evaded answering the question. They both snicker at the caught one and breath a sigh of relief.

Never make eye contact when the chaplain asks a question!

It is the same principle from former school days. The teacher asks a question of the class and a hand shoots up from the kids sitting in the front row who always are eager to answer. Most of the time, they do, relieving the pressure from those hunkering down in the back. But, every once in a while, the teacher breaks the patterns and waits for one of the skulkers to respond. This uncomfortable wait throws them into high, evasive gear as they begin their various maneuvers of escape and evading.

They fix their gaze on the shoes of the classmate in front of them. Gigantic football players suddenly contort their mass so they are hidden behind the diminutive girl in front of them. Any and all tactics are fair in this avoid-the-eye-contact-with-the-teacher-at-all-costs game.

This pattern is not unique to high schoolers. Those in the military who are in a saluting environment must master similar techniques. Saluting areas are places that commanders designate where the proper rendering of a hand salute is appropriate to senior ranking officers. In war, and in tactical areas, this is often forgone so as not to offer enemy snipers easy knowledge of who important targets may be. Camp Virginia is a saluting area. Soldiers are expected to render this military courtesy when encountering officers who out-rank them. But, there are ways around it when you are feeling obstinate, lazy, or just downright rebellious.

In this camp, with its dusty Kuwaiti streets lined by concertina wire and its oft-traveled routes to the chow hall (almost everyone eats in the Army, especially when it is free here in a combat zone), one cannot escape encountering saluting opportunities. But with a little ingenuity, one can avoid saluting. The key is to avoid eye contact. If this is successfully accomplished, you have got it made.

Lower ranking enlisted soldiers are particularly adept at this. One technique is changing your azimuth or direction of movement slightly so as to encounter the officer at a 45-degree angle. This considerably lessens the problematic eye contact. Another technique that works well takes more effort. Go into a fit of violent coughing and hacking a few feet away from the officer. Because of the frequent Kuwaiti Crud inflicting virtually everyone here, this wheezing is viewed as normal and no salute or contact is made.

Another time-honored method, used since Napoleon was a corporal, is to suddenly hear your first sergeant, commander, or even your mother, calling you over your left (or right) shoulder. This necessitates a quick and convincing jerk of the head to hear the summons. By the time one realizes their error, the officer is well past you and it is too late to salute. A truly excellent technique!

But, alas, almost all these methods of avoiding eye contact, and thus a salute, take considerable effort, and when it is all said and done, life is just easier if you simply go ahead and salute everyone to whom a salute is due, sort of like "Rendering unto Caesar what is Caesar's and to God what is God's."

Doesn't God deserve to have eye contact made and, in fact, desire to make eye contact with us? What is true in the military or the classroom or even during a sermon is true with God as well. Whereas eye to eyeball contact is essential to humans, God desires that intimate connectedness of the soul that when made requires a response.

Many go through life looking away or changing directions or avoiding face-to-face contact with God. Not believing or wanting a relationship with the eternal, they hear other voices calling, or go into fits of busyness when they hear God's call, having no desire to respond. They live in perpetual fear of losing control over their lives, of God taking away their fun, or God running their lives as the Superior Commanding Officer as they ignore, glance away, pretend to hear other voices, or get something in their eye and can't make that contact. They do anything rather than look into the eyes of the Almighty, for they know that if they do, they will be goners.

God, of course, might take away some of their fun or change their lifestyles considerably, this much is true. But, that does not seem to be the purpose of the God of the Good News of Jesus Christ. What God sees is his human creatures, made in his image, becoming slaves to a cruel and vicious tyrant that entices them into a trap and then uses and abuses them to death. Sin (the biblical word for rebellion and separation) and evil made eye contact with the human race in the Garden of Eden and it has been all downhill ever since that fateful day. Chains are what this tyrant offers us. They may be gilded and beautiful chains, but in the end chains are chains and only enslave.

If sin can make eye contact, so can God.

God comes in the form of God, Jesus the Christ, to make the contact that will change this entire world by changing human beings one at a time. God's plan is to live and die to break those hideous chains around our souls. God's Son hangs on a cross and instead of bringing down curses on the accusers and perpetrators, vowing revenge as his culture so easily encourages, Christ instead says, "Father forgive them for they know not what they do."

In the mother of double switches, Jesus takes on the punishment we deserve for our crimes and battles the forces of evil, giving back forgiveness, healing, and hope.

Jesus loses on that cross the eye contact he has enjoyed with the Father for all eternity so that we might be able to look into God's eyes once more and never be afraid of the Holy One again. From the cross, Jesus looks in his agony out on a broken world and in his nail-scarred hands and feet, he makes eye contact with God a reality again.

That eye contact is called good news. Then, to show us that it is really meant, the eternal Father in his loving gaze and by his magnificent power raises Jesus from the tomb to forever triumph over all that could possibly separate us from God again.

When you are walking down the street or wandering through a mall or shuffling through the dusty lanes of a Kuwaiti Army camp and you encounter a God whose love is so awesome and loving that he would die in your place, so that you could live forever in his place, please do not avoid eye contact with the Savior. He isn't interested in a crisp salute or a "Good morning, Sir," or even in a good, old, loud Army "Hooah."

What the Savior really wants is to look into your eyes and say, "You know, I really love you. Let me take your fears and pain. I want you to be part of my forgiven and redeemed family. And, it is all free."

For those who are sick of playing games, or shouldering a killing load of guilt and shame, or running their own lives and making a mess of it, to all who are humble enough to make eye contact with Jesus Christ, God has a gift today and for the rest of eternity.

Never make eye contact with the chaplain in a sermon?

Maybe. But, never, never avoid making eye contact with the risen Savior. In that encounter, your life will never be the same again and rendering a salute will not only be the least you want to do, but will become your greatest joy!

Recipe

Here's a recipe that everyone can easily follow at home.

Take a hair dryer outside on the hottest and driest day of the summer. Plug it in and be sure the setting is for "high heat." Before pointing it at your face, add a large fan behind it and turn it on to the highest setting. Next, add another ingredient: a winter heater turned on to the max.

Now, bask your entire body in the stifling heat for a good twelve to fourteen hours, occasionally shifting from front to back and cheek to cheek to get an even roast.

Just for added effect, turn on a bright light in your face as you bask.

Before starting the broiling, take a six- to eight-pound flowerpot, turn it upside down and place it on your head fastened by a chinstrap. Be sure to leave enough room in the headband for sweat to trickle out and down your eyelids.

Put on a heavy shirt and pants with boots geared to allow the minimum of air movement and then add a heavy winter coat or vest. Better yet, just for effect, put on a heavy corset and tighten.

Throw in front of the large fan, turned on high, at periodic intervals, a good handful of powdered sugar or flour so that it sticks to your body and clothes and on occasion throw a particularly large handful of powdery stuff so that it gets in your lungs and you can taste the grit between your teeth. If you aren't coughing up chunks of the stuff, you haven't thrown enough in front of the fan.

After basking, broiling, roasting your body, and wearing holes in your gluteus maximus for the prescribed length of time, stop in an area covered in dirt with the churned up consistency of talcum powder. Flop down on a cot under the full moon in the open and sleep the night away while trucks and Humvees hum around you all night long, throwing more and more talcum powder in the air while some sort of bug bites your weary, roasted flesh.

If you add all these ingredients together in the above said mix, then you can reproduce and feel what it is like on the first day of a convoy from Kuwait to Iraq. Not exactly the kind of details the U.S. Army puts in their recruiting commercials.

Moving from Camp Virginia on the "last COSCOM train out of Dodge" into Iraq was a memorable experience. MPs and transportation units do this regularly, but for the rest of us, it was a chance to see Kuwait and the Iraq that we were positioned against for so long in the Kuwaiti camps of the Army.

Camp Virginia gave us a nice send-off in a pleasant dust storm — a goggles-and-bandana-around-your-face sandstorm. But, once off the sand and gravel tracks of the camp, the driving was not difficult, in fact, it was almost normal driving on paved roads. One vehicle in our serial had mechanical troubles almost immediately, which delayed the convoy. We arrived late at our first checkpoint, a large, paved parking lot on the border of Iraq just south of the berm. Vehicles of every make and description were there to refuel either coming or going from Iraq. An Air Force convoy was there. Every vehicle had air conditioning. Every one! Why didn't I join the Air Force?

Crossing the berm — which is a literal ditch and wall of earth separating the two countries — we encountered a triple fence just before the berm into which our engineers had blown holes in order to let our troops through at the start of the war.

Immediately, we saw the kids begging and trying to sell colas. We could tell they were poor, not by their clothes, but from the adobe-homemade brick houses around the road. It was the kind of poverty I saw in Senegal as a missionary over twenty years ago. Very strict orders were given to throw nothing to these kids — not out of coldheartedness, but for their own safety. The more they are rewarded, the more bold their begging had apparently become, sometimes even stepping into the road to force a vehicle to stop.

Whether some were run over or not, I don't know, but the possibility was very great. A court martial awaited any soldier who threw anything to them. It's hard for Americans not to share, especially with children. But, sometimes safety is more important.

The road north was excellent — interstate quality. It was hot, but smooth sailing. Burned out tanks and APCs (armored personnel carriers) dotted the intersections. Dirt revetments were dug to protect in a tank-on-tank fight, but did little for attacks from the air. The pavement was scarred with baseball-sized holes, the obvious result of a cluster bomb dropped to take out Iraqi armor.

Surrounding all this were little farms of baked brick — not the red that is so common in the States, but a tan, mud-like brick that seemed to crumble easily from the looks of so many of these poor homesteads.

These must be the Shiites who had been so terribly treated by Saddam. There were flocks of sheep everywhere, donkeys, a few cattle. The land was terribly arid. Nothing grew that wasn't watered at the cost of great labor.

The first stopping point inside Iraq came at a military checkpoint which doubled as a refueling point. The constant military traffic and use of this area on the side of the six-lane road had turned the dirt into a light, powdery dust that was almost the consistency of powdered sugar. Every footstep, every vehicle, created a dust cloud that could not be avoided if you were downwind. One had to feel sorry for the poor young refueling troops who were forced to work and live in that mess.

Not long after leaving, we passed the area of the biblical patriarch, Abraham from Ur of the Chaldees. While we could not see the area that was supposed to be the ancient city of Ur, we could see enough to suggest the thought, "It's no wonder Abraham got up and left this place. He probably was jumping for joy!" Ur must have been much different 4,000 years ago, because it didn't look very inviting in 2003.

Not much later we crossed the Euphrates River. It wasn't impressive like the Mississippi or Columbia Rivers in the States, but how many times have we read in school history or geography about the Tigris and Euphrates Rivers where the Garden of Eden was said to have been placed by God?

Here we lost our smooth "interstate" and got back on mostly gravel and dirt roads — an interstate that never made it to completion.

A thunderstorm brewed in the west with flashing arcs of jagged light. Moisture isn't included in these storms, but the strong winds did bring plenty of dust and difficult driving as the light faded. Several times whiteouts made guessing where the road might be and where the vehicle in front of you might be the driving method of choice.

Before the light disappeared, shepherds and poor rural families lined the roads. Some begged for food with the universal motion of hand-to-mouth hand signal while others held knives to sell along with cola drinks and an occasional liquor bottle of some sort of "hooch." It's a good thing that general order number one forbids all alcoholic consumption.

An exhausted group of soldiers refueled, ate MREs (Meals Rejected by Everyone), and before long set up cots next to the vehicles lined up in march order for the next day. The facilities were "in the weeds" — just like at Boy Scout Camp.

A full moon appeared after the storm clouds passed south of Baghdad and the long first day of the convoy was over.

At first light we heard something we never heard in Kuwait — not gunfire or anything military. Those are sounds all too familiar. What we heard was a rooster at first light. Several soldiers suggested shooting him, but the convoy commander said he was just doing what he is paid to do — so leave him alone. Because of the benevolence of the commander, he lived to crow another day in Iraq.

A quick brush of the teeth, a little swipe of a baby wipe across the face, and we are gathered for a short convoy brief before starting out again. MSG Morrison, the senior NCO and chaplain assistant gave the essentials about staying closed up in towns, not throwing food out to those along the road, and getting out and providing security in case of a breakdown.

LTC Steve Larson, the convoy commander, addressed us all with a safety briefing that normally accompanies any military movement ... except this time it was with an emotion-edged voice: "If I had my choice today, I'd be home with my family. My son graduates from high school today ... but, because I can't be home, you are my family and I want everyone to get home safely. So be careful as we drive. Let's get there safely."

The words came hard for him as the emotion came to the surface. Many of us could empathize. The week before, my daughter graduated from college and I missed celebrating my twenty-fifth anniversary with my wife all in the same week. They aren't easy milestones to miss at any time, but it seems especially poignant when in a combat zone far from home in the Middle East on a convoy with a group of soldiers that have become your family to one degree or another. No one can replace those whom you love most, but every soldier can identify with the difficulty. Some days are just harder than others and not just for soldiers far from home, but those back home as well.

Soldiers face a blessing and a curse when it comes to their emotions. By nature and by training, we keep our emotions hidden, under wraps for the sake of not letting them cloud our judgment when we must make cold and rational decisions in war. We can do that most of the time except for allowable venting sessions usually aimed at the confounded and unfathomable ways of the U.S. Army.

We need to express our emotions at times, yet the military culture frowns upon it. There are times when even the strongest of characters can't keep their feelings suppressed. It comes boiling to the top, creeping into our voices and eyes. Strangely, the very soldiers one thinks might disapprove, understand. A rousing hand of applause was given for Steve's graduating son.

Soldiers need those moments to again be human instead of cogs in a great big impersonal military machine doing a hard job, to remember for a few moments in a dusty field surrounded by Humvees and Deuce-and-a-half trucks that we aren't made of stone. Those things we value most, the most important fundamentals in the deepest places in our souls ... are not things at all, but people: our families, our hometowns, our comrades, our nation.

We can endure the separation and missed milestones only because we believe in carrying out our duty for the sake of, and the safety of, those we love most — our desert family in camouflage in front of our eyes in Iraq and more importantly our families far away, back home.

The biggest change on the road the second day was the green — not Army green, but genuine vegetation green, something that we in Kuwait hadn't seen much of the last few months. In the dark of the day before, we had passed from arid lands with sheep and camels to rows of palm trees and irrigation ditches, bigger farms and houses with numerous animals, to a more prosperous area than southern Iraq.

Again the six-lane highway was crowded with primarily military convoys going north and south although the civilian traffic picked up greatly as we drew closer to Baghdad. There were few private cars, but many older U.S.-made Suburbans, custom vans, and eight-passenger vans, all used as taxis taking people toward Baghdad, dressed mostly in western dress, with a few in traditional garb.

Numerous ponds in the process of evaporating dotted the roadside. People in several of them gathered together the evaporated remains into white piles of salt ... regular "Morton salt girls and guys" although the salt had to be somewhat gritty. I wonder how they get the dirt out of the salt?

Kids were taking flocks of sheep out to pasture, some leading the sheep that followed obediently, while other flocks walked forward leading the shepherd.

North of Baghdad, one little girl caught my eye. She was about seven or eight years old and was followed by a string of about twenty sheep. She wore a pretty, bright blue dress, had a scarf-covered head, and had the prettiest smile on her face. While she walked along, she waved to us in a pleasant, constant half-arm wave. I'd have given anything to stop and take her picture, but of course, that is a "no-no" in a convoy. Such a pleasant, friendly sight she was.

Several times, we saw what must have been married women, tending to home chores and waiting for transportation along the highway, who were dressed head-to-toe in black, "nun's habit-like" clothes although their faces were not hidden as in pictures one sees from Afghanistan. Those waiting along the highway stood in the hot sun separated from men who were, of course, all seated in the shade. No chivalry there, at least not by Western standards.

The traffic increased as we got closer to Baghdad and began to skirt the city by way of a beltway that took us through stop-and-go traffic. There were few overt signs of war. Every once in a while there would be what must have been a government building that was bombed, but it was hard to tell if this was recent or from the first Gulf War.

Every vehicle that went by us or was stopped next to us in traffic seemed to stare or look at us, but not with unfriendliness. Many waved, especially when we waved first. Heaven only knows what we in the United States would do if a conquering army invaded our land and cities, and then inundated us with troops and vehicles.

But I never saw a defiant or angry gesture — at least one that I recognized. We passed a long line of cars — at least a mile long and two deep. People were obviously waiting for something. Many just pushed their cars forward in the queues. They turned out to be waiting in an incredibly long line for gas.

I saw a sign with Saddam's picture painted on one side, but the other had obviously been wiped out.

We went by another line at the Saudi humanitarian relief station where they were passing out food. A giant mosque greeted us as we got near the airport turnoff and then we were on the north side of Baghdad.

What we saw throughout the city was again reminiscent of any third world country; small shops, trashy by our U.S. standards, but seemingly industrious. Some of the vehicles that people drove were amazing for their obvious age and being beaten up in third world traffic. Most of us would never even give our sixteen-year-old with a new license, a beater like those. Farmers bringing their produce to markets that were along the road, seemed to drive the worst vehicles. Saddam must have never had any farm support programs so they could buy their own 4x4 pickups.

Watermelons, sheep (live and skinned out carcasses), vegetables which were all mouthwatering after the food we had been eating for months, filled these roadside stands. We sped through the city to the north past what must have been barracks of the Republican Guard. A giant howitzer guarded the entrances to these vast facilities. As we came to know it later, that military area was Taji, a favorite target of insurgent roadside bombs and RPG attacks.

Burned-out Soviet-made tanks littered the roadside as we got farther north out of Baghdad. Finally, after driving four hours, we got to the gate of our base known as Anaconda. It was a short day compared to the day before, but very interesting in the variety of people and experiences. Most of us don't get off the base and it was well worth it this initial time.

I hope this narrative can help folks back home have a slightly better understanding of what their soldiers are doing, experiencing, and looking forward to leaving behind whenever the order comes to redeploy out of Iraq.

Thanks To Freedom:
Shukran, Shukran

"Thanks to U.S. to freedom. Iraq, 6-18-2003." He wrote these words on a 250-dinar note of the Central Bank of Iraq. Saddam's "pleasant and peaceful" picture figured prominently on one side. He had a regular "George Washington" look on the bill that was bluish in color rather than U.S. dollar green.

The Iraqi who wrote these words was a civilian translator at a U.S. Army base not too far from Baghdad. We were at the chapel trying to get a recalcitrant civilian air conditioning unit to operate in the intense Iraqi sun that already beat unmercifully though officially it wasn't even summer, yet. It had been consistently between 110°-120°F degrees every day and on the weekends when various congregations of the base chapel gathered to worship, it had been more of a sweat fest than a hymn fest.

As chaplains we always hope to have a red hot sermon and fired up worship, but it has become more literal than spiritual of late. The translator assured me that come August it will be 120°F in the shade and not just out in the sun as it is now. Oh, brother, that is something to look forward to ... NOT!

We will find out the truth of it, for most of us know that we will not be going home prior to then. As I stood in the mid-morning sun around the air conditioning unit watching the two other Iraqi men working on the electronics of the system and wiping sweat from under my desert boonie cap already sweat-stained and damp from the exertion of standing there, I asked the translator about his life.

He was a thirtyish, single man with a degree in civil engineering, and a large extended family. He had wanted to take his degree outside the country during Saddam's reign to work in order to support the family, but the tight control of the Iraqi state would not give him his degree. He could not prove that he was a civil engineer without it so he was trapped with the education, but unable to use it because the dictator held control over his sheepskin.

He didn't explain why this happened. I surmised that like any totalitarian state, control is everything; they don't have to have a reason. Make people "toe the line" wherever the elite and powerful decide to draw it and for some reason that makes them happy. Perhaps he was not rich enough for an under-the-table payment to the right person to free up his degree so he could go abroad to pursue his dreams. His hope now was that by working for the Americans he could survive long enough to find a job in the post-Saddam Iraq with U.S. help.

He talked about his hopes for his country, saying that America must stay here long enough for the people to overcome over thirty years of being totally controlled by the state and to be able to start thinking for themselves, to think as a free people, yet with responsibility for the welfare of every clan and group. "That will not be an easy thing to do," I said from my understanding of how difficult it was for the Eastern bloc people in Europe to overcome a fifty-year legacy of deadening communism. "Habits are hard to change and most people would rather be miserable in a comfortable habit than to take the risk of trying an uncertain but more promising future."

Yet, we as Americans can't rightfully be too hard on this new struggle of the Iraqi people. How difficult will it be for a nation that has no experience in democracy to suddenly become a modern, functioning one? Americans and the media want it to emerge today, but history tells us that it did not even develop in our own country that swiftly. Freedom's habits and institutions take time: years, not months.

Despite the heat, meeting this Iraqi citizen was a refreshing experience. We read and hear about the hard-core Iraqis who are still fighting to resist change, who want a return of the murderous dictator, who fear freedom's song. They had it good under the despotic rule of one of their own, despite the sufferings and mass graves of the majority of other Iraqis, and they will seek to continue to kill to keep it that way.

But there are so many other Iraqis who want to breathe freedom's air of hope and opportunity. It will be a tortuous process. We Americans have forgotten democracy's struggles because we remember so little history and take for granted so many of our rights and freedom. American democracy was far from a sure and gloriously certain principle in the early years of the republic in the late eighteenth century. It took time with many battles won for the people and, to be sure, many battles lost along the way, endangering the people as well.

I was reminded that many, many Iraqis are grateful for the chance to be free and if nothing else good happens through Operation Iraqi Freedom, may this be our legacy to the people of this nation: the chance to be free, to live as a free people. There are no guarantees, however, and it will most likely be a major miracle if democracy takes root anywhere in the Middle East.

But, miracles do happen here. One actually occurs before our eyes when the ailing air conditioning unit jumps to life and we all celebrate by standing in front of the cool air vent, soaking in its pleasantness, shaking hands, even as I repeatedly stumble in pronouncing the only Arabic word I know, the one for, "Thank you." "Shukran, Shukran," I mumble. They all laugh at my pitiful attempt at a Semitic language, but they understand the universal feeling of gratitude.

Thanks, indeed, for the coolness, for the fixing of this piece of equipment. But most of all, thanks that two human beings from differing worlds, one in desert camouflage wearing a cross, one in blue jeans and a Muslim; one from a conquering and occupying democracy; another from a defeated dictatorship, yet a proud people, can connect and understand the human yearning for freedom, peace, and laughter.

The translator moves away from the cool air and prepares to jump back into the Humvee guarded by two young soldiers from an engineer unit in North Dakota, good, old midwestern boys. He pulls out of his wallet the 250-dinar note with Saddam's deceptively placid picture on it and as his pen refuses to work in the hot sun, I offer my trustworthy, purple PaperMate pen.

He writes on the bank note words not seen in the mass media much, but appreciated by hot soldiers far away from home and very tired of it:

"Thanks to U.S. to freedom. Iraq, 6/18/2003."

To one Iraqi, at least, freedom's sweet song and cool breeze is hopefully just beginning. To an American soldier, it is a powerful reminder to pause long enough to say "Shukran, Shukran" to the generations of Americans gone before who enabled him from birth to breathe this sacred and refreshing air of freedom.

"Shukran, Shukran" in the blazing Iraqi sun or at the Independence Day picnic or any place we breathe this rare and precious air so highly bought by the blood of so many Americans.

Shukran, Shukran.

Razor Wire

It is everywhere in this military camp.

What was commonly known as "barbed wire" is now "razor wire" or otherwise known in Army circles as "concertina." The "barb" of classic barbed wire that farmers and ranchers typically use for their herds has become a more menacing, thin slice of razor-sharp metal.

It comes in rolls and is strung out quickly, but only with a pair of thick, leather gloves. Sometimes, it is uncoiled on the ground without stakes to support it as if sending a message from a finger-wagging mom or a teacher saying, "Utt - ut - uhhh! Don't go there. Don't even try it!"

At other times, the razor wire is anchored on posts and is two or three layers high which definitely sends a more ominous message, "Hey, buster, don't even think about coming this way."

On a morning run in this former Iraqi military installation, one can see razor wire laid out in pockets everywhere. Every unit puts it up around their headquarters, sleep and chow areas, and sometimes, even around latrines. ("We don't want people we don't know defecating in our facilities" seems to be the message there. Or, it could be they are also guarding their toilet paper — a far more likely scenario.) In any case, the wire adds a measure of security to sensitive and valued areas or items.

It is definitely an effective means of controlling access and assets. Only the most determined of would-be attackers would try to breach these wire obstacles. It can be done, of course, and combat soldiers from sappers to infantrymen know how to do this. But pilferers, thieves, and the like would not attempt to go through such hazards and usually move on to easier pickings. After all, who really wants to tackle razor wire unless there is an absolute necessity for the sake of life, liberty, or the accomplishment of the mission?

For most of us, the wire does its job. There is no combat necessity to breach this obstacle. It then effectively keeps less-determined people out of areas that the owners of the wire don't want them into.

All over this installation, there are small enclaves surrounded by this effective obstacle.

As a pastor who can't think or see anything without asking, "I wonder if I can use this as a sermon illustration?" or "How I can get a children's sermon out of this?" it dawned on me while jogging past one such wire enclosure that this truly is an illustration of the Good News of Jesus and of many people sitting in the pews every week.

The "wire" takes us back to the ancient Jewish temple with its progressively restrictive zones as one goes deeper into the worship areas leading to the innermost sanctuary, the holy of holies. These zones religiously and figuratively speaking put up razor wire barriers to more and more humans as they progress inward.

As a Jewish believer entered farther and farther into the temple, access became more and more narrow from the outside to the innermost center of the temple; more and more limits were added based on "who" you were ethnically, and what you were socially, which were usually dictated more by the accident of your birth than the depth and commitment of your faith.

The Court of the Gentiles where non-native Jews could proceed in the temple but no farther, displays one such restriction. The next constricting area was the Court of Women where female believers could worship, but must stop on pain of death at the boundary.

Each layer was spiritually like razor wire, double- and triple-strand wire laid out, doing its job of restricting and denying access to a deeper, closer relationship with God.

Then came the Court of Men, where the razor wire forced all Jewish males by birth, except the Levite priests, to proceed no further. Only those priests of Levitic birthright could enter the innermost rooms of the temple, but even they must all stop before the holy of holies, all except the high priest who could enter just once a year.

A new layer of deterring razor wire was added at each level, effectively denying spiritual and literal access to more and more of God's people ... until Jesus the Christ came.

Imagine for a moment in your church, triple-strand razor wire around the altar keeping all sinners away from Holy Communion, away from communion with God where you could see and sense God's presence, but you could not commune intimately because you happened to be born a Gentile, or woman, or in the wrong tribe or nationality? It is not a very pleasant thought for most of us who yearn for a loving embrace from our Heavenly Father.

Yet sin, that old rebellious nature deep in our souls and human genetic makeup, does in effect erect such a barrier to a loving and holy God. Its razor-sharp barbs cause us pain, shame, and guilt that keep us away from the healing, wholeness, and forgiveness we desperately need.

And in the Christian faith, we believe that God hates this as much, if not more, than we do.

His plan in the beginning was not that we should be separated from his love, but that we would embrace it and wallow in its eternal richness. But, in fact, our wrongs and human willfulness have kept us apart from his love and erected barriers that we cannot overcome no matter how hard we try.

An often-overlooked verse in Mark's account of Jesus' death on the cross tells us what God's intention has always been toward his lost creations.

> *But Jesus, with a loud cry, gave his last breath. At that moment, the temple curtain ripped right down the middle.* — Mark 15:37, 38 (The Message)

The witness of scripture tells us that Christ has broken down the walls and razor-wire barriers of separation between us and a loving, yet righteous, God.

In military terminology, Jesus' death "breached the wire, overcame the obstacle, and cleared the way" for God's troops to move through and into the deepest corners of fellowship with God the Father. The cross was more than the unfortunate death of an idealistic Jewish carpenter. For Christians, it was God himself, "Emmanuel — God with us," ripping down once and for all time the wire around his presence, his house, his eternal kingdom. Jesus' sacrifice destroyed sin and death's power to keep us away from God, for in Christ we have been cleansed, washed clean of the guilt of our wrongs, and welcomed into the family of our loving God.

One version of the origins of the word "fellowship" records that the word has nothing to do with "fellows" — good old boys drinking coffee over cake and cookies while leaning their rounded stomachs on the table. Instead, "fees" were small parcels of pasture in England where shepherds over the centuries had gathered stones together to separate their flocks. But when two shepherds trusted their neighbors, they demonstrated it by breaking down the walls between their "fees" and allowing their flocks to comingle, establishing what became known as "fee-lowship."

Whether this is true or not in word entomology one can only guess, but it sure is a great story that illustrates what God has done for us in his Son. He broke down "the dividing wall of hostility" as Saint Paul wrote, that kept us at a distance from holiness and love. Now, in Christ's death and resurrection and the destruction of the barriers, we are invited into a progressively deeper fellowship with the God who loved us this deeply.

Never again ought any obstacle of ethnicity, gender, lay, or clergy distinctions separate us from our Heavenly Father (Ephesians 2:13-14).

The wire around the altar is gone forever and all are welcome to meet and receive this God in the word and in the bread and wine of Holy Communion.

But sin's razor wire formerly separating us from God's presence is not the only place barriers appear in life. We, as individuals, place plenty of "razor wire" around our own personal lives as well.

In the same way the ancient temple was walled off to deeper intimacy with the Almighty, we as individuals do this with others. Here is an apt picture of all the little protected areas, exclusion zones, that we create for ourselves, areas walled off not just to God, but to keep others away from the real inner core of who we are on the inside. They are sensitive areas, vulnerable zones where we hurt too much or the wounds are still open and festering; where the shame, the guilt, the fear is too great for us to allow anyone near who can see the pain, the shame, the festering putridness of our brokenness.

How many times have we so innocently stepped into "razor wire" when talking to family, friends, or acquaintances? Without a clue, we stumble into those tender zones and receive a sharp, biting response. We ask a simple question, make a completely innocent comment and we are suddenly met by a rattlesnake coiling and rattling away. The message is clear: "Stay away or suffer the consequences." In an instant, the razor wire is up surrounding them and we stumble away bleeding, bruised, and wary.

We stagger away from the encounter asking, "What in the world was that about?" We never saw it coming, yet the wire was there, razor sharp and doing its job, keeping all from peering inside to see their unbearable pain. In no uncertain terms, the message was delivered and a sign squarely posted, "Off Limits."

As a pastor, I couldn't begin to add up the number of times this has happened through an innocent comment, a benign joke, or just being in the wrong place at the right time. Whatever the case, I was there and they unloaded.

It is only later, sometimes years later, that enough clues and perspective were gained to come to some understanding of why this or that person put up such protective wire refusing access to all.

We all have these wire enclosures in our lives. The places we don't want others to see, the places where the hurt is too deep, the guilt and shame too powerful. We are afraid that if others see us as we really are on the inside, we will, indeed, be alone more than ever, that no one will understand, that the vulnerable side of our lives will be scorned and held up to ridicule by all who see our bared souls.

We convince ourselves that it is better to be alone than to be rejected, better to trust no one than to be betrayed, better to hide than to take the risk of opening up to clean out the festering recesses of a wounded, hurting soul.

Yet, razor wire is not just for the hurting as a self-defense measure. It is also used to protect personal power.

The insiders of any organization, the old-timers who have the reins of control in their hands also put up razor wire around their prerogatives and power. Better that they and they only are granted access to the inner sanctum than to allow newcomers to bring change and new ideas. "We've never done it that way before." "We've tried that before," "When you've been here longer, you'll understand."

After being repelled at this wire, most take their bloodied efforts at contributing their gifts, new ideas, new ways of doing God's will and retreat to a place they can serve God wholeheartedly and with welcome.

We are so adept at putting up barriers, magnificent, really, as humans. It comes so naturally, so easily.

But God is pretty good at tearing them down, too, and has had a lot of experience at doing so.

That is why the tearing of the curtain in the inner holy of holies of the ancient temple seems so small, yet has such great significance.

What separates us from God is destroyed in Christ's seeming defeat on the cross. What keeps God away from our secret lives and wounds is forever torn down through the bloodied body of the Savior and his victory over sin, death, and the evil one.

Jesus falls on the razor wire so that we can step on and over his bleeding body like soldiers breaching barbed wire in an old WWII movie. The sacrifice of the one allows all to get through the barrier and bring victory to what had seemed impregnable and impossible.

So, maybe we should ask ourselves where the razor wire enclosures in our lives are and why are they there?

Are they from past wounds? Guilt? Shame?

Jesus will bring healing, forgiveness, and wholeness.

Are they erected so we can keep our neat little worlds and personal fiefdoms intact without the interference of God or his will?

Jesus will break down every barrier no matter how well fortified or how old or rusty the razor wire.

Is the wire up to protect others, to keep others from harm, like a fence on a high crumbling cliff? If so, that is the only barrier that God allows — one that protects and defends others out of love.

Razor wire is everywhere here in Iraq, but among God's people wherever they may be, our Lord enjoys knocking down every barrier that isolates, festers, and kills his children of faith rather than protects and guards them.

And that is a lesson you don't have to travel to Iraq to learn.

> *[Christ] has broken down the dividing wall, that is the hostility between us. (Saint Paul)*
> — Ephesians 2:14 (NRSV)

Mass Hug

It appeared to be the military's version of a hug, an unintended one, but still a visual mass hug.

It was a hug of soldiers, by soldiers, to each other at the death of a comrade in this combat theater of operations called Iraq.

They were lined up in a large, dusty rectangle encased by sandbagged tents covered with camouflage netting. The red unit flags stood at each guidon's side, the "castle" insignia of Army Engineers flapping gently in the Iraqi wind on this warming July morning.

Soldiers in desert camouflage uniforms (DCU) with weapons slung over their backs stood in a formation before a flatbed trailer functioning as a stage. Many had water bottles protruding out of leg cargo pockets as protection against the oppressive heat of even a mid-morning sun.

Each engineer company formed a portion of an elongated "U." What was unusual was the mass formation of soldiers in the center of the "U." They were a company of soldiers from North Dakota, the unit that had lost a comrade in an ambush just a few days before.

This was a military memorial ceremony for a National Guard soldier who was the first from his state to die in combat in the Iraqi war. Fellow engineer units and individuals came to support them and share in their grief and sadness. Surrounding them, each unit formed extending, embracing arms around their fellow hurting engineers and soldiers. They communicated by their presence the care and respect that only comrades-in-arms who have shared the burdens and dangers of war in a foreign land can understand. They, too, know and share this loss of one of their own.

It appeared to the observer to be a loving, understanding hug, a military hug, the same kind of hug that is seen in countless funeral homes and churches back home as loved ones and friends embrace in mutual support against the pain and heartache of loss.

The colors of the nation flew in the morning breeze as the young female company commander spoke of the soldier she had come to know well since being mobilized, the unit's chaplain sounded the hope of Christ in the face of the apparent hopelessness of death, the brigade commander described his admiration for all the gathered soldiers, their bravery, their willingness to sacrifice so much to give a foreign people the hope of freedom and a measure of justice for the first time in centuries.

Each speaker in their own way pictured a thirty-year-old soldier from North Dakota who volunteered not once, but three times, to be part of something bigger than himself and paid for that willingness with his life.

Scripture was read, a young soldier played his guitar and sang a song he wrote for his lost friend. It was a touching tune with words of friendship, the willingness to stand in harm's way, and the willingness to serve. Later he sang, "On Eagles' Wings" — a prayer from Psalm 91 for all, but especially for the young wife left behind to pick up the pieces of her life and somehow go on living despite what a war 7,000 miles away has taken from her, forever.

The entire formation was called to attention for roll call, the remaining soldiers from North Dakota and soldiers from around the nation in active or reserve units all stood at attention. Names of living soldiers from the company were called and they responded as they would normally, "Here, First Sergeant!" Name after name was called, each echoed with, "Here, First Sergeant!" ... until the missing soldier's name was called. Silence. Again his name was called, more silence as the enormity of the loss sank deeper into the assembled soldiers. One final time, the complete rank and name was called, and with the final silence, the first sergeant ceased to call out.

The haunting sound of "Taps" began.

Few sounds grab a soldier's soul like that melancholy bugle sound. All were at attention, not a muscle moving, with eyes staring forward or downward. The only movement was the tears that could not be commanded to cease as American soldiers in a "U" formation, "hugged" living comrades by their honor and respect while saying good-bye to one of their own in a foreign land, all wondering if this soldier's sacrifice will bring hope and freedom or be squandered to another ruthless tyrant.

No one on that Iraqi morning knew the answer. They could only pray, shed their tears, salute their fallen, and then soldier-on for the sake of their comrades, a widow, a family, a state, a nation.

The mass hug disintegrated at the dismissal into another hot, Iraqi morning to keep carrying on at their appointed missions as American soldiers in Iraq, even as one of their own went home to North Dakota.

The Rivers Of Babylon

By the rivers of Babylon we sat and wept when we remembered Zion.   — Psalm 137:1 (NIV)

It wasn't until I stood by one of the rivers of Babylon, that this Psalm had any special meaning for me.

It had been just another sad song of lamentation from a sad time in the history of the people of the Old Testament, but not one with much meaning for today.

I realized how wrong I had been as I stood by the waters of a canal from the Euphrates River, gazing at the ruins of the ancient city where Daniel, Shadrach, Meshach, Abednego, Ezekiel, and other heroes of the Bible faithfully served God. These ruins are contrasted in modern times by a palace overlooking them built by Saddam Hussein, the man who apparently thought of himself as the new Babylonian emperor and successor to Nebuchadnezzar.

The ancient site of Babylon is located in Iraq, south of Baghdad just outside the city of Hillah. The war against Saddam Hussein has presented an opportunity for many soldiers, sailors, and marines to visit the place that was the center of world attention and power 2,600 years ago and the subject of so many biblical stories read in Sunday school and in worship. U.S. Marines are now headquartered around the ruins of the ancient city that once was an empire that brought fear to ancient lands, an empire that figured so prominently in the Old Testament.

In 600 B.C.E., Babylon was the world power that few could resist. Its armies controlled land from what is modern-day Iran throughout all of Iraq, up to Turkey, and down to the Holy Land of Palestine. The Old Testament records how God repeatedly sent his prophets first to the divided nation of Israel, to the northern kingdom and Judah to call for serious changes in doing justice and being faithful to their God, but repeatedly the prophets were ignored, rejected, and even killed (2 Chronicles 36:15-21).

The power that ruled what the Greeks called Mesopotamia, destroyed the walls of Jerusalem and the most potent symbol of God's presence, Solomon's temple. They slaughtered masses of

Hebrews leading off the best and brightest of Judah's population to exile in Babylon. Psalm 137, like many Psalms of the Hebrew songbook, is a song of lament — a sad song akin to, but more dreadful than, many a country and western song of loss and pain. Its anonymous singer recalls a bitter memory of a lost homeland far away, with little hope of return. It is a song of the pain of the defeated, a mocked people describing the torment of their captors.

Then, in the psalm comes the difficult question that reverberates even to our day and time in a foreign land as soldiers,

> *How can we sing the songs of the Lord while in a foreign land?* — Psalm 137:4 (NIV)

This is a good question and one that many a soldier is asking this day stationed in, around, and by the rivers of modern Babylon.

Most soldiers have been in this combat theater for six months or more. The separation from their families, friends, and homeland has been a 24/7 experience and everyone at home and in the theater are tired. The uncertainties of war, its dangers, potential and immediate, its exhausting, but boring, pace have given way to stabilization operations with the inevitable two steps forward, one step backward.

The war is over, but it is not.

The job is done ... but it is not for so many, and those who anticipated a joyful, sooner-rather-than-later reunion back home are now resigned to the fact that it will be later, rather than sooner. A weariness, a daily trudge, has set in among troops who eagerly listen for the latest rumor of redeployment dates, but who have also come to trust little of what they hear and to believe nothing until the day they are told, "Pack your bags and board the plane."

How can soldiers here in Iraq and loved ones back home sing the songs of the Lord in a foreign land? How can we sit by the rivers of Babylon and not continually weep for home? There are no easy 1-2-3 steps or lessons here, but we are also not without some things we can do.

The ancient Hebrews, even in their misery and oppression, were assured by God that this captivity would not last forever.

This, too, will pass and, in fact, the Almighty would see that God's people would return home one day. The exiles in Babylon had to remember this promise even as they wept in their separation from all that was familiar and loved. They would one day come home, God promised, but it would not be immediately.

Like children waiting for a birthday or Christmas morning, there was to be anticipation, but from now until the dawning of that long awaited joyful day, life must be lived fully. The future must not be waited for at the expense of the daily duties of life. Keeping the routine, getting through one day at a time, is the salvation of those on a long journey whose conclusion seems so endless and far away.

We, as soldiers and waiting families, must keep moving day-by-day, step-by-step. A busy and tired mind and body will not dwell so readily on the unpleasantness of the wait, one that can only be accomplished by keeping in the thick of the daily grind.

Then, the exiles in ancient times were told to seek the good of the place where they were led in chains by their oppressors. The prophet Jeremiah (29:4ff) tells the defeated Hebrews to continue to live life as fully as possible, even in their captivity. Speaking for the Lord, he tells them to

> ... *seek the peace and prosperity of the city to which I have carried you into exile. Pray to the Lord for it, because if it prospers, you too will prosper.*
> — Jeremiah 29:7 (NIV)

Those ancient people weeping by the rivers of Babylon were not to spend all their time in self-pity or misery. Instead, they were to do their best wherever God planted them, even doing their best for their enemies. It is not exactly an "if you can't beat em, join em" attitude, but it is close.

Few of us can control our circumstances in the Army at this point. Our choices are either to get depressed and defeated by circumstances we do not care for, or we can decide, "Well, I'm here. I don't like it, but I'm going to do my best and make the best of this until it is over."

105

Then the final thing exiles, ancient or modern, must do is to remember the promise of hope.

Jeremiah, a few verses later, sets out hope for those far from home with no redeployment date in sight. Again speaking for the Lord, these words are words to recall every day:

> *For I know the plans I have for you, declares the Lord.*
> *Plans to prosper you and not to harm you, plans to*
> *give you hope and a future.* — Jeremiah 29:11 (NIV)

We will come home. We will make it through the heat, the separation, the tears, the frustration, the trials. And, if we do not refuse to get up and drive on, trusting that there is hope after weeping at the rivers of Babylon, we will make it as we support each other and not turn on one another in our frustration. We will make it as we live our daily lives fully, even though we are not whole, far away from our loved ones. We will make it as we communicate with and encourage one another, helping each other to get through another day, another month, by reminding each other of the sure hope of the day when the bags will be placed on the plane for home.

It will be then that we gladly modify the ancient psalmist's words in our own personal way and pray words that are short, but profoundly meant:

"By the rivers of Babylon, O Lord, we serve."

Thank you for bringing us safely home to sing your songs among those we love and in a land we love.

Army End Credits

Are you the kind of person who leaves the theater before the end credits of a movie are shown? Or do you stay and at least look for the screen name of a character in the movie or to find out where scenes in the film were actually shot?

Depending upon your answer, you may or may not be able to understand what soldiers in the COSCOM really do every day in Iraq and Kuwait.

Most people identify a movie by the headline actor or actress who is the star of the film, "Yeah, you mean that movie where Tom Cruise was _____? Or the one with Sharon Stone where she played such and such?"

That's what makes a star a star. We remember them.

But who was the key grip or the best boy or the wrangler in those movies?

Beats me. Who cares?

Well, we ought to care, because there would be no star, no Tom Cruise, no Meg Ryan, without hundreds of people whose names are virtually ignored as the credits of the movie are rolling at the tail end of the film.

When's the last time you looked closely at those people and their functions? Probably rarely, if ever, and yet, there would be no movie and no stars without the contribution of *all* of those people doing unnoticed, small, but vital jobs to bring the film to the big screen.

Who's the art director, the storyboard artist, the key hair stylist, the head carpenter, head painter, translators, negative cutter? The B-camera operator, gaffer, best boy, the dolly grip, foley artist, and the focus puller or key grip?

Most of us have no idea what these people do, much less pay any attention to their names in our favorite thriller. But, by adding their skills together in a giant group effort, we either see a great flick we really like or feel ripped off by a real "dud" of a movie.

With the help of a few internet sites, one can at least have an inkling what some of these film terms and jobs are and their importance.

A gaffer is the chief electrician or lighting technician of a movie. Who'd have guessed that? The best boy isn't a boy at all, but the gaffer's first mate or second in command. Grips grab hold of things, but are really the crew members who move and assemble equipment on the set. The chief of the grips is called the key grip. A focus puller adjusts the focus of the camera, and foley artists create the incidental sound effects that help us interpret the scenes we are seeing.

Surely there is an interesting story behind all of these terms. But this is not a class on filmmaking as much as it is a way of comparing the function of logistics soldiers with that of the hard-working behind-the-scenes artists, craftsman, and laborers of the film industry.

The thousands of soldiers in the 3d Corps Support Command rival in variety, complexity, and sheer numbers their film making brethren. Yet the common thread in both cases is that stardom and recognition are the farthest thing from their thoughts.

The soldiers of this high-stakes Army movie in the Kuwaiti/ Iraqi theater are the quiet worker bees of the end credits. They are the ones who plan, organize, and direct everything that supports the stars, the fighters, the ones who make the evening news and the Army recruiting posters, as well as the morning papers back home.

A Pentagon general recently dropped the COSCOM from his schedule of units to visit in Iraq because he wanted instead, we are told, to visit the fighters — the combat divisions. The infantry, aviation, and tank troops definitely deserve all the attention they receive and more, but it is just another example of logistics soldiers being forgotten back in the end credits. The truck drivers take on just as much danger as the fighters do in today's Iraq.

However, let people run out of toilet paper and then watch all the attention that the "loggies" will suddenly receive — none with a smile. Beans, bullets, showers, vehicle parts, transportation, and a thousand other insignificant (rest assured that no soldier considers toilet paper insignificant), but vital items are what COSCOM soldiers are about. Some plan and most others execute those plans.

But you will rarely, if ever, see their names in the headlines of tomorrow's *Washington Post* or *New York Times*.

That is, of course, all right with most soldiers, as long as someone, sometime, somewhere recognizes their contributions, sacrifices, and importance to accomplishing the mission for the nation.

A popular story of the last few years illustrates this point. The story is called "Who Packed Your Parachute?" A Navy pilot who was shot down and bailed out over Vietnam had plenty of time to think as a POW. In captivity, he began to consider the seaman on the ship who was responsible for packing his parachute the day he was shot down. Who was he? He didn't even know his name. What if he hadn't taken his job seriously? What if he had a bad day, a hangover, or didn't care, and just plain decided not to finish packing that parachute correctly, thinking no one would notice, no one would really need it — not today, anyway?

The pilot returned from his captivity and wanted to know who that sailor was so he could thank him, realizing that his life depended upon this insignificant crewman who would never have the fame of being a Navy pilot or star in a movie like Tom Cruise in *Top Gun*. A little-known, seemingly small job and yet without it, this pilot would not have lived to tell about it.

The same could be said in less dramatic terms of members of virtually every human organization from churches to VFWs to the Girl Scouts. Who are the people inhabiting the end credits of those organizations without whose contributions, faithfulness, and skills everything else would have fallen apart or self-destructed? What if they suddenly decided that they no longer cared, no longer would add their skills and gifts to the group, or do their tasks well unless they got some recognition and glory along with the stars?

The results would not be good for individuals, organizations, and society. Logistics soldiers inhabit the end credits of the military, but the Army would not be able to shoot, move, communicate, or do all the other essentials in war — without the daily work, sacrifices, and skills of these nameless troops.

The next time you watch a movie in a theater or even at home from your DVD player and television, take a few extra moments before you run to the bathroom or gather up your belongings off the sticky, syrupy, theater floor coated with spilled heart-clogging showtime popcorn and watch the end credits. Look for the gaffer, the key grip, the best boy and read their names.

And as their names pass over your lips and bounce around inside your brain, think this thought over: "I'll never meet you face to face or shake your hand, but thanks for what you did to make that an enjoyable movie for me to see."

In showing gratitude to them for their contributions, let your mind wander 7,000 miles to Iraq and Kuwait where you'll find the Army's end credits — key grips, gaffers, and best boys. The seemingly faceless, but hard-working, danger enduring, freedom loving logistics soldiers are doing their inglorious jobs day after day; always in the background, with little or no accolades, medals, or press releases; not packing parachutes perhaps, but feeding, clothing, transporting, and supplying those who will be quoted in tomorrow's newspapers or will show up on the evening news.

If you can recall these young and old "Army end credits," then you will be thinking of, praying for, and being grateful to soldiers of the COSCOM and understand what they are all about in this hostile fire zone called "Iraq."

BOG Is Real, But So Is Serenity

Hello from our portion of Iraq.

I thought, perhaps, a general letter to the Family Readiness Group, family and friends back home might be appropriate instead of the usual story.

Most know by now that our unit and *all* active and reserve soldiers in Iraq have been involuntarily extended to "365 BOG in Iraq."

As you may have guessed, the office of official Army acronyms, hidden in a secure area deep within the bowels of the Pentagon, has been very busy during this war and just recently has given us this new term, BOG, which means "Boots On the Ground."

This is the Army's way of saying, "Y'all in those boots in Iraq will be staying right there for at least a year before those boots and the feet contained therein will go back home."

Many soldiers are more than willing to donate their second pair of desert boots to stay on the ground in Iraq while transporting their feet and connected body parts back to the States, but alas, the Army, swift as always to sniff out a GI scam, has seen through this ploy and extended BOG to the second pair of boots as well. Oh, well ... nice try.

The fact of the matter is that soldiers in general and reservists in particular are disheartened right now about this extension, not to mention how their families waiting back home are feeling. Because of their orders and the regulations that govern redeployment, reserve units believed that at most they would be in active uniform for a grand total of 365 days, which meant that a vast majority of reservists would be out of Iraq sixty days ahead of their final demobilization date and thus home for Christmas (early December).

Such was the early plan and hope, but as our commanding general is fond of saying "The enemy gets a vote," and their actions have caused this unwanted extension. So we will be singing "Silent Night" and "Grandma Got Run Over By A Reindeer" in Iraq this year, and there is little hope of that changing.

While people are disheartened at the moment (even soldiers have a right to be disappointed, don't they?) very few are crushed by the news of BOG. Enough hints and rumors abounded in previous months to alert those listening that this might happen. When the official word did come, it was saddening without doubt, but not the surprise, crushing blow it would have been without prior warning.

The next three months, though, until after the holidays, *will* be the hardest on soldiers and their families.

Time will drag. The upcoming holidays will heighten the sadness and remind everyone of what they are missing. We have to acknowledge that, plan for that, manage that. The chaplains and stress-control teams here will most likely be doing landmark business and families back home should be talking to their pastors, counselors, and trusted friends about their struggles and feelings as well. We will all need to pull together and help each other get through this time.

The thing is, though, we will all make it through this, whether stateside or in Iraq. Troops and families will adapt and overcome. A saying that has become one of my favorites is "Blessed are the flexible, for they shall not get bent out of shape."

We all need to be flexible now. It may not be with a smile on our faces, but we must drive on, do our jobs, do our duty, and make the best of a situation completely outside of our control. Otherwise, we will bend our lives completely out of shape and when it is all said and done, we may never recover the shape we desire. Many know the Serenity Prayer and its wisdom:

> *God, grant me the serenity to accept the things I cannot change, the courage to change the things I can, and the wisdom to know the difference.*

These are powerful words, wise words for this crazy, mixed-up world. But, this is just the first part of the complete prayer. There are more powerful, wise words to it that are rarely printed on plaques hanging on our walls, words that may help us deal with BOG and a thousand other unpleasant situations in life.

In 1926, Reinhold Niebuhr penned the first, familiar lines and these words, less known, but crucial for our situations:

> *Living one day at a time. Enjoying one moment at a time. Accepting hardship as the pathway to peace.*

Taking as he did, this sinful world as it is, not as I would have it. Trusting that he will make all things right if I surrender to his will; That I may be reasonably happy in this life, and supremely happy with him forever in the next. Amen.

Living one day at a time — the only way through a long road march or journey is to keep moving one step at a time. The only way through a long wait is to simply live one day at a time, getting through each day, each week, not weeks or months, but simply one day at a time doing as the old saying encourages, "Making each day a masterpiece."

"Shred, spindle, mutilate" your free bank or farmer's co-op calendar. Use it for cat litter or starting the fire in the fireplace. Don't look so far ahead that each day's joys are lost in longing for what you are missing so that the days have no joy, no promise left to them.

Enjoying one moment at a time — soldiers and families can't put their lives on hold waiting for better times. Too much precious life is lost. Keep your routines, enjoy the little things of life, children and grandchildren, ballgames, concerts, movies, and popcorn. Hopefully, those routines won't be quite as much fun without your soldier or loved one beside you, but life goes on. Each moment of laughter is a gift. Don't squander it. Enjoy all you can until they can be shared again with your soldier.

Hardship — can make us bitter or better. I've never seen a bitter person enjoying life more than those who turn lemons into lemonade. Bitterness sucks the joy out of living not just for yourself, but also for those around you.

Most bitter people are like B-movie zombies — the living dead. They look alive, but inside there is nothing. God is an expert at helping people become better through hardships and struggles — even when the separation is 7,000 miles and 365 BOG. God simply requires us to help him out by being willing to let these difficulties make us better human beings.

God, after all, has dealt with more difficult hardship cases over thousands of years than this. Let us allow God to teach us how to be better people — to grow, be more independent, trusting, self-assured, confident, and more in love with our spouses and families than when this all started back in January 2003, taking the world as it is; not as we wish it to be.

Hollywood is full of fantasy, but most of us have to live in the real world. We can't close our eyes and wish it all to be different or even kick and scream about it not being right or fair. It might feel good to unload our emotions for that twenty or thirty seconds, but in the end it doesn't change much.

The fact of the matter is that BOG *is* and that is all there is to it. It is not as we would have it. But let's not waste precious life and energy beating our heads against brick walls. The Army has thicker walls than any of our heads. (The Army has some pretty thick heads, too! But that is a different letter.) Trust and surrender are the key actions for us all in making it through BOG, not finding hope in a human institution, but trusting that God is still on his throne despite the U.S. Army, terrorists or war; trusting that God will make all things right, that God can bring good out of all this so that we may be reasonably happy until BOG is completed.

We learn soon after high school that this is not a perfect world. Few things are ideal. Dealing with BOG is a matter of being as happy as we can reasonably be under the circumstances: not perfect this side of heaven, but as good as normal human existence can expect.

I apologize that this has turned much more into a sermon than I intended, but then again, what else would you reasonably expect from the chaplain?

And if that prayer didn't help you much, try this one titled "The Stress Victim's Serenity Prayer":

> *God, grant me the strength to eliminate from my life*
> *the things that can be eliminated, the serenity to deal*
> *with the things I can't, and the wisdom to distinguish*
> *an act of stress reduction from a felony.*

May God give us all the grace and strength to handle BOG so that we may be reasonably happy while living each day fully and finding some measure of God's joy along our boggy Iraqi paths.

An Iraqi Day — Burn Detail

Imagine waking up to the sight of morning bonfires in the gray dawn or slipping into a sweaty cot with the flickering flames of more bonfires in the evening dusk. So serene, so idyllic sounding from a distance until one realizes that those bountiful bonfires are really sawed-off 55-gallon drums full of diesel fuel and human excrement put to the torch.

Welcome to another day in Iraq.

This daily burning ritual is familiar to all soldiers at this sprawling base north of Baghdad and likely known in every unit location in this occupied country where U.S. Army troops work, live, and sleep. In fact, one cannot escape the flames and smoke as they rise in the wind above the base. One just hopes that the wind is blowing away from your billets and hanging so the smoke and odor do not linger in your nostrils, tent, or clothes for very long.

That is but one of the mundane elements of life for soldiers in Iraq not often experienced in the land of flush toilets.

While the variety of soldier experiences here are too wide and diverse to lump into a single theme that every soldier would recognize, there are many common elements, the "Burn Detail" being the most unique of these commonalities. It is almost comical to watch those tasked with this unpleasant detail of Army life. In our unit, the task is assigned by enlisted tent, so, for a whole day, they have the privilege of holding their noses, pouring diesel fuel and watching the sacrifice to the Pentagon rise.

Some seem to make the best of it. They bring their fold-up lawn chairs bought in Kuwait and sit around the burning drums like they were having a campfire over the Fourth of July weekend. With Gatorades and Cokes in hand, they sit around, talk, and watch the flames. Admittedly, they don't sit too close to the campfire or roast any weenies, but they seem to allow their imaginations to supply what is obviously lacking.

The obvious advantage of the detail is that you have no other details to do that day. In essence, soldiers can relax watching the you-know-what being incinerated.

The other day a group from the 76th Army Band, "V Corps' Finest" sat in such a relaxed configuration. Walking up to them, a chaplain commented that he doubted that the band members would ever have dreamed that they would be sitting around such a fire talking and laughing rather than playing their musical instruments. The irony was as thick as the black smoke.

For most 3d COSCOM soldiers and other units here, life in Iraq is somewhat, but not completely, like a stateside military base. Most officers and senior NCOs live in buildings with varying degrees of repair or disrepair. Enlisted soldiers live in military tents which have electricity, refrigerators, and fans. Not surprisingly, the tents are green and dust-colored ovens during the day. But at night the air is often far cooler in the tents than around the buildings, making sleep a much more viable option.

What definitely doesn't work anywhere at the moment is the plumbing, so there is no need to worry about bathrooms, indoor showers, or commodes. Those are all outdoor activities just like at scout or Bible camp, the hunting lodge, or granny's house in the country. There are no porta-johns with all their bright colors and relative privacy. Those for the moment are the things one dreams of back in Kuwait. Here there is no one to pump them out, thus the daily burn detail. It's plywood facilities or nothing and nothing is not a decent option.

There has been some excitement among burn-barrel watchers in the last few days. Several trailer-sized shower units have arrived from somewhere (most likely Kuwait), been installed, and hooked up.

Well, sort of, as there is yet one small problem. No one has been contracted to fill the water tanks. So there they sit like a Christmas present under a tree and there is still a month to go before Christmas.

Showers are available through an Army bath and shower unit where standing in line for anywhere from a few minutes to 45 minutes can get you a whole seven minutes of water. (Men get seven minutes because there are so many. Women get unlimited minutes. Where is the gender equity in that? Jessie Jackson, where are you when we really need you?)

116

Needless to say, few men spend time singing in the shower. Women singing? Don't know and ain't gonna find out.

Others shower using the solar water bags that are common among outdoor enthusiasts. These bags when put out in the sun transfer the heat to the water and *voila* you have hot water for a shower. That is not really necessary here because the water is warm all the time anyway from the hot sun. In fact, finding cold water to drink is the trick here.

Shower stalls have been constructed by many units so that the solar bag is hung high and a quick shower is available. There is no dawdling and no letting the water run while you soap. It is 1) wet down, 2) soap up, 3) rinse off, and 4) hope that you haven't miscalculated the volume remaining to rinse off completely before running out. The hard fact of life is this: Once it's gone, it's gone. Period. End of H$_2$O.

It is rather surprising, however, how little water it takes to clean up. We waste so much water back home. But when your soldier gets home, don't be surprised if they indulge themselves a little and linger in the shower longer than ever before. Maybe, just maybe, it might be long enough to hear a little singing while they are at it.

One also has to be careful when showering here in the shower bag stalls. Most are out in the open so that half of creation can watch a person shower. Sidewalks run nearby, convoys park only fifty feet away in one direction, Humvee parking is just fifty feet in the other. Of course, the plywood is strategically placed so only the head, lower legs, and shower shoes can be seen (just ankles and shower shoes on less tall soldiers), but if you drop your soap as many of us are wont to do in the course of a normal shower, the consequences can be quite revealing.

Murphy's Law dictates that, "If anything can go wrong, it will, and at the worst possible moment with the greatest possibility of disastrous results." The corollary to this law for shower stalls is: "Any dropped soap bars will automatically bounce at a direction and a distance from the stall so as to be just outside the reach of the naked owner." Well, modesty is not a soldier's best friend in a combat zone.

"Wanna do your soldier a favor?" Send them a bottle or two of liquid body soap. This cuts down greatly on the probability of the bouncing-outside-the-stall in front of a fifty-vehicle convoy bar of soap phenomena.

Drinking water is now provided through a quartermaster water unit which necessitates daily runs to the water point to fill up the five-gallon cans (they are actually plastic now, but who's being technical?). Bottled water here, we are told, is to be a thing of the past, although many of the areas quartering soldiers in Iraq still must use bottled water.

Each day, water is transferred from the cans to canteens and liter-and-a-half bottles for drinking, with troops usually adding Gatorade, Kool-Aid, or other instant flavorings. Of course, it is also great for coffee, for shaving, for solar showers, or hand washing the clothes. Most soldiers still do their own washing, although a military laundry unit is taking some bags and returning most of the items the bag originally contained.

So goes a day in the life of a soldier in the Army at just one base inside of Iraq. Depending upon editorial discretion, watch for further possible installments of *Life in Iraq* like "Army Food — To Eat or Not to Eat," or "Chow — Not Breakfast for Supper Again!" and "Rumors — The Soldierly Art of Self-Inflicted Misery."

No Hooah Zone

If there is one sound you are liable to hear almost universally around the Army, it is not that of a Humvee humming down the road, or a helicopter hovering in the distance, or even formations of gray and black PT-uniformed soldiers jogging through the gray and dusty dawn of an Iraqi morning.

The ubiquitous sound, the one heard more often than any other in the U.S. Army, is the sound of "Hooah."

One can't exactly call it a word, really. It is more of a guttural sound somewhere between a human grunt and the sound a squealing pig. It comes close to being an intelligible word, yet this one five-lettered utterance (four-lettered if one goes with the short spelling) conveys a vast array of meanings.

It is used so often by so many soldiers in so many situations that one almost hates to hear it again. In fact, in one office at this large American base north of Baghdad, a sign on the wall expressed the feelings of many a good soldier concerning a good thing gone wild. The sign was of the universal symbol for something prohibited: a circle with a diagonal line through it, and a bold caption below it reading: "No Hooah Zone."

Some Army soul was surely sick of hearing that sound/word once too often and finally snapped, creating a sign befitting his feelings, because Hooah has become an all-purpose way of saying, "Yes," "No," "Okay," "Ja!" "Ya betcha," or all of these rolled into one. This concise grunt is heard constantly throughout the day.

Now, this two-syllable sound's meaning all depends upon the user's context and voice inflexion. As in the English language when two words often sound the same, only from the context can you tell what spelling and meaning are intended.

"There" and "their" is one example that drives most of us berserk in writing. They both sound the same, but one indicates a place and the other possession.

So with Hooah. It can be a straightforward, "Yes, Sir" to a question. "Do you understand the mission, Sergeant?" "Hooah, Sir!"

Or when asked, "How many of you soldiers want hemorrhoids?" "Hooah" — said in a low tone without much volume can mean "No way! Not in a million lifetimes, First Sergeant."

But a "HOO-O-O-O-O-AH" in a loud, sustained roll would reply to a question of, "How many of you want to go back home to see your family?" The answer to that particular question would indeed bring a loud, long, exuberant guttural response by troops here in Iraq.

Unfortunately, that prospect has been smashed in the last few weeks here in Iraq, and now a much more somber, "Hooah," spoken without gusto or enthusiasm has been the norm. It is more of a quiet, "Hooah" spoken in response to the query, "Okay, do you all understand the situation when it comes to redeployment?"

"No Hooah Zone" might be the sign that expresses the feelings of a good many mobilized soldiers at the moment. The hope of going home soon, or even by Christmas, is now officially gone and the new theme in the Army is BOG.

No one can say for sure now what the actual redeployment date will turn out to be, but the gusto is definitely gone for many.

Whether a perfunctory or an enthusiastic, "Hooah," is in order, or none at all, soldiers here will keep marching on, doing their best to do their duty ... until they can all break out into a loud, long and sustained, "Hooah," when they are told to pack their duffel bags and head for the plane.

So for a few days or weeks a "No Hooah Zone" will be just fine with most reservists in Iraq. And then, they will drive on, day by day, even if the holidays are hard pills to swallow.

But if some sound is required, there is surely this all-purpose Army word in which some variant tone can match any somber, hard occasion.

"Hooah" — not a zone, but an attitude. (You supply the tone, emphasis, and style that fits your feelings today.)

Anaconda Chapel

Camp Virginia Chapel

Outside chapel in Kuwait

Altar made from crates

Saluting a fallen comrade

Praying at a memorial

LTC Kittleson preaching

Eli's Christmas tree

Easter Sunday Communion

LTC Kittleson with local family

LTC Kittleson with local children

Local children

LTC Kittleson and local child wearing Kittleson's helmet

LTC Kittleson with school children

Mousetrap

The mouse lay there glued to the cardboard, literally glued.

It was in a trap, simple, effective, somewhat crude, but it worked.

I heard it in the night; a strange noise in the Iraqi night. It was eating a peanut still in the shell, a peanut some nice American sent to a brave soldier fighting for their freedom in Iraq.

Now, how could I have an insurgent, Iraqi mouse eating food destined for American soldiers? It just wouldn't seem right. So I decided to do my humble part in the war on global terror and bring this dastardly, sneaky no-good free-loader to justice.

A peanut in the center of the trap is the bait. One step onto the cardboard spread with a sticky type of superglue and the mouse is stuck.

First one paw then the other. The more it struggles to free itself, the more body parts get stuck until it is lying prone on its side, stuck from head to foot and completely immobilized except for a pitiful squeak.

At first, one might feel some sympathy. Surely, I could spare a peanut or two, and my room is plenty big enough for another living creature. It's just that the sanitation part is irritating. After one cleans up all the mouse droppings of an active rodent, all sympathy dissipates.

Thus, the mouse becomes mired in its own cravings, dies because of it, and I have no pity.

Human beings on reflection can be very much like mice. We could even mention John Steinbeck's classic title and story *Of Mice and Men.*

We, as humans, end up in the same deadly predicament because of our desires and the different deadly baits of life. Our western culture, for instance, is mired in the happiness bait.

This bait proclaims that life, in all of its parts, exists for one goal only and that is to ensure my happiness, my feelings of well-being and pleasure; that happiness is what life is all about and whatever I do in this world should offer me this elixir or else.

We kill ourselves to buy things to make us happy and they do ... for a few weeks or a month or two until we grow accustomed to them, take them for granted and begin searching for that elusive feeling of happiness all over again. We have become hopeless happiness junkies.

The bait does its job and after a few steps, the glue does its job — all too well. We become trapped in this constant feeling of un-happiness, so we buy more, trade in older spouses for younger ones, older cars for newer ones, a bottle for human relationships. We become more deeply trapped in cycles that always promise true happiness, but never deliver.

Finally, one day after trying it all and becoming weary of the endlessly unfruitful quest, we squeal out much like the pitifully trapped mouse, the words of the teacher in Ecclesiastes:

> *Meaningless! Meaningless! ... Utterly meaningless! Everything is meaningless.* — Ecclesiastes 1:2 (NIV)

A Trust Of Life

"I would trust him with my life."

The commander spoke softly, but with a great dignity with which the gathered soldiers could easily identify.

"I could say he was a good soldier, a friend whom we will miss," he continued, "and that would all be true. But I can say nothing greater than 'I would trust him with my life.' "

The young commander sat down, but his words keep echoing in our minds ... "Trust him with my life, trust him with my life."

The memorial ceremony in a bombed-out hangar in Iraq would seem a strange place to hear such reflection, but the brief, powerful words were understood by all the soldiers with uncovered heads and close-cropped military hairstyle. They had come to pay their respects, to gain closure, and to hear words of encouragement and hope. Those were all present in the chaplain, the commander, and the friends who paid tribute to one of our own who had fallen so recently.

Most did not know the young sergeant whose life was taken from him on an Iraqi road by a hidden bomb. Soldiers who knew him best spoke poignantly of his life and their grief and pain. The words "miss him" were repeated over and over again. Tears flowed, as this is one of the few times, culturally, when soldiers are allowed to embrace and cry without shame or embarrassment.

Their friend and comrade who shared the danger of daily life here won't be going home to a joyful reunion, at least on this earth.

Yet, for the majority standing in that Iraqi morning with weapons slung over their backs, their presence is not due to close friendship with a soldier killed in action, but simply because he is a soldier like themselves and they have all come to a deeper understanding of what soldiering means.

One can go to a thousand Memorial Day ceremonies in America and no matter how magnificent, how grand, how well they are done, those who are far away in time and place from the dangers of combat or shared fear while doing their jobs can never truly understand what it is these soldiers with bowed heads in reflection are experiencing deep inside.

There are a million different thoughts, of course, among them, but it seems that the cement, the glue, that binds soldiers together in danger, is precisely what the commander said.

"I would trust him with my life."

That is exactly what 18-year-olds and 23-year-olds do in Iraq every day.

The piece of any solitary soldier's view is too small to see the big picture, if anyone truly can. They do what soldiers throughout the ages have done to make it through life's most common and tragic event — war. They do their jobs day after dangerous day, relying on each other, their friends, their comrades.

Fortitude and courage do not originate in grand patriotic speeches or even superior firepower (although most troops would take their chances with firepower), but they come from hope and from devotion to each other as comrades.

The "hope" is that dawning day when they will take off their Kevlar helmets and chin straps and drop them to the ground for the final time or fling the bulky flak vest in a corner or turn in to the arms room their constant companion of every waking moment of every day overseas — that M-16A2 rifle. The hope to once again embrace the loved ones they left behind and the life they are eager to regain.

That is the hope that keeps soldiers going.

And "each other." They have learned that in life, but more particularly in war, no one makes it alone, no one does it all by themselves; everyone needs other people, friends, buddies, those to whom they can entrust their lives to, those who, like them, share the misery, the danger, the laughs, the tears, the cussing, the complaining, and the joys.

Every day these American soldiers put their lives in the hands of their God, but also in the hands of their brothers and sisters in arms who reciprocate with the same fierce devotion to each other's welfare and safety.

When those cords are broken in battle, in an instant in an ambush, a piece of every soldier suddenly is missing and all feel the loss. They come; they come to the memorial ceremony of a soldier they never knew, but whom they can infinitely respect because that soldier, even in death, was someone whom you could trust your life to ... a fellow soldier.

Only now can those troops standing silently with heads bowed understand their grandparents, parents, uncles, and cousins; predecessors in war, who stand tall despite the erosion of time on their bodies on a windswept cemetery in any town America on the last Monday every May and amid the flying flags and the speeches remember deep in their soul a long lost friend, a comrade from World War II or Korea or Vietnam to whom they trusted their lives: someone who did not return alive again to their native soil.

And when "Taps" begins its melancholy sound at the end of the ceremony and a tear flows down that old weathered cheek as he wrestles with his battles, demons, and griefs of long ago, never again will these young American soldiers look at those tears as the weakness of old, sentimental men.

Instead, they will know without hesitation that the old veteran is remembering his buddy, his friend, his comrade to whom he would and did entrust his life in some godforsaken killing field around the world decades ago.

It is not so strange then, that this commander would say so few words and yet have said it all of this fallen soldier because that is what soldiers must willingly be and willingly do every moment of every day in this place called Iraq.

"I would trust him with my life." There is no greater compliment and gift from one soldier to another.

Tikrit And Perspective
(Or Dodging Bat Guano
In The Iraqi Dusk)

We were sitting on the veranda watching Bradley infantry fighting vehicles roll by as clouds of burning fecal matter drifted across the sky from the daily ritual offerings of the U.S. Army in Iraq. We've seen the vehicles of an army in war clatter by hundreds of times as they come and go down the four-lane street renamed "Pennsylvania Avenue." It is a daily ritual, but every once in a while a surprise appears to make us take notice.

Such a surprise came the other day when someone saw a Massey-Ferguson tractor rolling down the avenue driven by a soldier in desert camo and Kevlar helmet. Bouncing along like any farmer in Iowa heading to the back forty, it really grabbed our attention in contrast to all the military vehicles we see.

One of the more famous trucks at LSA Anaconda is a cargo vehicle with a sign in the front window that says "One Weekend A Month, My _____" (body part expletive deleted).

Obviously, it belongs to an irate reservist or national guardsperson exercising his First Amendments rights who would certainly like to meet their recruiter again for a little tete-a-tete discussion. Part-time soldiering seems at the moment to exist only in recruiting commercials.

Cooling off on the veranda of the ALOC housing, the supply, personnel, inspector general, and chaplain sections of the COSCOM headquarters, the last vestiges of a 120F degrees-plus day dissipates. But those gathered to chew the fat do not just watch vehicles drive by or observe 55-gallon drums of burning human waste. (Oh, just a bit of advice, make sure that you do your best to walk upwind of these burning smudge pots. The reason should be self-evident, but walking on the correct side is not always possible.)

We at the COSCOM administration location also have the privilege of watching the bats come out of the roof of our building. About dusk each night, they slide out by the drainpipes (that drain nothing most days) and fly away in search of insect victims. Our only danger sitting in our fancy plastic chairs is the bat fecal matter that occasionally flies our way.

Sitting here in Iraq one can easily meditate on keeping life in perspective, particularly with the lack of other entertainment options. In general, thinking is not a time-honored Army value and a tricky thing to do, but in order to make the best out of a less than desirable situation, it is really essential.

The other day, several of us got a chance to go to Saddam's hometown of Tikrit about eighty miles north of LSA Anaconda. Observing how other units are living, as well as the Iraqis, is a good thing because it puts our own situation and lives in a better perspective.

Everyone, including troops here, have it relatively better or relatively worse than someone else, no matter where you go. An Army support base in what used to be the Iraqi Air Force Academy outside Tikrit seemed to be on par with our base. The main difference was that the region is much drier. (Remember how amazed we were coming up to Iraq from Kuwait and actually seeing green vegetation? We'd not seen green for so long that even the green scum and algae in the stagnant pools of water looked good.)

It doesn't take long as one pulls away from the river basins before the desert and dry conditions take over the countryside. Crossing the Tigris and its irrigation canals, one could look to the right as we traveled north and see the land between the rivers with its green vegetation and verdant fields. But to the left of the road, the country quickly turned into a brown and lifeless looking desert. In fact, the scenery and heat made us think we were again in Kuwait.

The Tikrit support base was just as sophisticated as Balad's, but in a much more sparse area with little vegetation, yet there was at least one distinctive. They had a DFAC (mess/chow hall) tent that amazed all of us from down south. Here is where perspective returns.

Get this! They had hamburgers that tasted like real-live meat. Honest to goodness meat!

We all looked at them in awe — for about two nanoseconds before grabbing them and digging in. Real ground beef, not like our normal soy burgers (with a touch of sawdust for consistency) from our base. (We wondered if they were Saddam's cows. If they were, "Too bad, too sad. Not!") And they had four, I said, four (that's almost as many digits as most soldiers have on one hand) different kinds of salads. We couldn't believe it. Real meat, real salads, and all in one day, one meal. Amazing.

Perspective.

To top our perspective meter, we were offered chocolate chip cookies that weren't dry and hard, but rather cool and moist. The taste buds went berserk. Eating like that made us not even notice or care that we were eating in a fest tent again, especially when we didn't have to stand in line for twenty minutes in the noontime heat to get in.

When you're eating back in "the land of the big salad bar," keep in mind that if you can count the number of salads in the salad bar and then add up to more fingers than you've got on one hand, then life is good, very, very good.

It's all a matter of perspective.

Later we went down to Saddam's palace along the Tigris River in Tikrit. We aren't talking one palatial building or one palace here. We are talking a sprawling complex of many palaces that can't be counted on the digits of both hands and feet. While this area was new to most of us traveling in the IG Humvees, I must say that there are people in the COSCOM who were here a long time ago and have seen far more and know far more of the area than we, but for us, it was certainly something to see.

The Fourth Infantry Division is headquartered in Saddam's palaces whose opulence is both amazing and infuriating. The marble and textured designs and walls were beautiful, the spaciousness amazing. It was incredible. But it was infuriating to realize that all of this was built just for one man, his sons, and their cronies.

There was nothing here for Iraq or the people living in poverty; just for the "new Nebuchadnezzar." How sad, but dictators are always about raping and pillaging their people for their own self-glory, not the citizens' welfare. The view of the Tigris is great over the bluff, which was ironic for many of us at LSA Anaconda, as well. For three months we have lived not more than a half mile from the Tigris River and have never seen it. We are pretty much confined to the base for security reasons, and sightseeing is not the leisure sport to be engaged in at this point in Iraqi history.

To see the Tigris at Tikrit from Saddam's palace was another perspective event. This is a place of history.

A final lesson of perspective was (back to the bodily function thing again, sorry) porta-potties. I wrote several times about various aspects of life with them at Camp Virginia in Kuwait. Since leaving Kuwait, we also left behind our plastic friends that we all loved to complain about. Upon coming to Iraq, those were just sweet memories to leave behind. (Pardon the pun.)

But on Saddam's Tigris bluffs, we found some porta-potties and you'd have thought we'd all seen the crown jewels for the first time. How sad is that when a bunch of soldiers consider it a big step *up* to use a porta-pottie? Yes, life is a matter of perspective. Someday, we may even get to use a real live flushing commode, although we will need to bring along some bottled diesel fumes just to feel at home.

The next time you begin to feel sorry for yourself concerning the struggles of your situation, take a good look around and get a wider view of things. There are some who are better off and in palaces with non-diesel-fuel-smelling porta-potties.

But, most people have just as many challenges as you do, and perhaps a few more, that even on our worst days we wouldn't wish on our worst enemy.

And yes, some people have real meat in their hamburgers and a bean salad or two more than we do, but we aren't all living on the edge of a desert and not many people can watch good old Iowa tractors plod by or dodge bat guano in the simmering Iraqi dusk.

Life is perspective, and life in Iraq, or life while waiting back home, is definitely what you make of it. Once a person opens their eyes to look beyond their own navels, they may see challenges as opportunities to grow as human beings.

A Dash Of Mustard

All of a sudden my vision became a blurry yellow hue.

Momentarily confused by this hitherto unknown experience, it took my brain a few nanoseconds to process this event in DFAC #1 (mess hall, chow hall, salmonella salon, road kill: Middle East, whatever) at LSA Anaconda, Iraq.

I was used to my glasses getting splashed, that is for certain. It happened a few times even on the way to the mess hall. Our experiences of intense heat and dust covering everything have changed to moisture and mud on our installation. A good rain the night before turned everything that wasn't asphalt or gravel into a mushy, oozing, chocolate brown mud. Vehicles speeding by on what is known here as Pennsylvania Avenue (no president's home on it, though) pick up and spit back out in radiating circles voluminous globules of mud, eager to attach itself to any and all soldiers within splashing range.

So, brown splotches on my glasses are becoming normal. But yellow ... that is a different matter.

In the jam-packed DFAC, a young female soldier sat down at the one vacant seat next to me on the crowded table of hungry lunchtime soldiers. She had a normal GI lunch of a couple of soy burgers and French fries. Her condiments were, likewise, the usual catsup found in a pan one must ladle onto plastic plates and mustard which is only found in individually wrapped packets.

One of the first tasks of eating here in Iraq is to open everything that you need in order to make the meal more palatable. Ripping the straw off the orange juice or milk container (milk that can be without refrigeration for up to ninety days) just like in a Juicy Juice for kids back home, one must usually struggle to overcome the plastic covering over the straw. Sounds simple, but more often than not, exertion resulting in grunting, groaning, pulling, shredding, and/or mutilating must be performed before the straw is liberated and useable. Obviously, it shouldn't be that difficult, but when one realizes that Murphy's Law is the first and foremost of Army regulations, it isn't all that surprising.

After the straw liberation is accomplished, wrapped packages of butter, jam, or catsup are next in liberation order until all the extras that make an unpalatable meal edible are accomplished. The young soldier next to me was doing just that when I felt the splat and my vision turned murky yellow, much like a bug splattering on the windshield in the summer.

It isn't a lot of fun to get splattered with mustard any time, but particularly so in an Army mess hall far from home where washing facilities for uniforms are called buckets and the agitator is one's hands. She, of course, had no intention of "assaulting a superior ranking officer with the intention to mustard them." But accident or not, it is not a particularly good idea in the Army for a private to splatter a lieutenant colonel with any sort of condiment, much less mustard. But, as they say, "Stuff happens."

Yet, an amazing thing came from that mustard attack. Rather than cursing, threatening, or name-calling, a conversation arose.

She apologized, of course, and then looking at me said "No offense, Sir, but I don't trust preachers."

Pausing and curious while smearing mustard further over my glasses in a vain attempt to clean them, I chuckled and said, "I can't say as I blame you. I don't like preachers much myself. You obviously have been wounded by some."

The private then expressed how in the past several toxic encounters with clergy had left her deeply hurt, and after listening while munching on the noodles and beef on my plate, I could understand why. I would have felt the same in her shoes.

People in church almost always love Jesus, but Jesus' followers often leave a lot to be desired. We can be a hopeless bunch of judgmental fanatics over the most insignificant issues, driving needy, fragile believers away from the very group God has assigned to nurture and help their faith to grow. Such was the case for this poor woman. Not once, but twice, she had been let down by holy leaders. Ouch! After a while only a fool would allow that kind of hurt to be repeated.

I told her that I often ask people who have been hurt by churches and pastors if they like to eat out. "Do you like to go and eat out at restaurants?"

Puzzled, she said, "Sure, Sir."

"Well, here's what makes sense to me. When you've eaten in a restaurant and gotten a horrible meal, what do you do? Do you decide not to return to that restaurant again? If you're wise, you do. Or do you decide never to eat out again concluding that all restaurants are bad? Most of us keep eating out, but try different places until we find one that provides a good meal that makes us want to return for more."

That word picture seemed to hit home.

"Pastors are human," I said above the roar of hundreds of other talking soldiers and the constant activity by the ice cream bar across from our table. "All have their weaknesses and their strengths, but they are not all the same. There are plenty of decent pastors and churches. Don't give up. You rightfully have a sour taste in your mouth, but there are good restaurants out there, lots of them; none perfect, but still good for you and your faith. We all need a restaurant to feed our souls for this tough journey we call life. Few of us make it safely to the end all alone."

We talked some more until my boss finished his ice cream. She seemed glad that we had talked. At least, I was.

Picking up my plastic utensils and the plastic plate cluttered with empty milk cartons, napkins, and leftover gristle from my Swiss steak, not to mention conquered plastic straw wrappings, I left saying, "Keep looking for that restaurant. God has one for all of us."

"Thanks, Chaplain," she said, "I'll always remember that."

Maybe she will, maybe she won't.

What amazes me is not our conversation, but how willing God seems to be to use the truly trivial, just plain irritating, if not infuriating incidents of life to bring some grace to a generally graceless world. He uses them to teach and to bring a little portion of meaning even to the most mundane events, as well as the truly profound. And for those who are willing, even the smallest mustard packet (seed) can be used to bring about something good.

That isn't to say that we search for opportunities to get mud or mustard thrown in our faces. Life seems to provide those free of charge on a regular basis. But when they splat our way, what will we do with them? Blow up in a tirade at someone who is responsible? Or allow God to redeem the irritation and bring good by turning the irritation into something productive and life affirming?

There are plenty of days, of course, when getting splattered with either mud, mustard, or both, leads to responses that are anything but grace filled, responses with plenty of heat, but little light and even less precious peace. In fact, that is probably the norm for us rather than the exception. Hateful glares scream silently, "You complete idiot. You dumb so and so" explodes off our faces and through our eyes; expressions and thoughts that no clergyman is supposed to express, much less think.

But the "Old Adam," the sinner within every redeemed heart, is still very much active and evident. We know theologically that its power is diminished and ultimately conquered by God in Christ, but until heaven, it is still very much present for duty. We are not proud of this old nature, we hate it in ourselves in our more sane and calm moments, but it is still there and is all the more easily exposed as minds, souls, and bodies become tired, stressed, and worn by separation and anxiety. It wears on and wears down our fragile souls, only to pour forth in a mustard moment.

But every once in a while even in Iraq while eating at the "only restaurant" in town, God tries once more to use his children, we sinner/saints, through a small packet of mustard, to communicate something very important to one of his struggling children of faith. For that, we can only offer an amazed prayer of thanks.

Lord, help me wherever I find myself this day to be gracious enough and secure enough in your forgiveness and love through Jesus, the Savior to take a dash of mustard across the chops and see in it an opportunity to deliver a bit of your voice to a needy, hurting world.

God has surprises everywhere we go, and his promise is as good now as it was 2,000 years ago when a jailbird apostle called Paul wrote: "Now we know that all things work together for good for those who love God ..." (Romans 8:28 NRSV).

Jesus said his followers are to be the salt of the earth (Matthew 5:13). I honestly never dreamed that we could be mustard as well.

But It Hurts, Sir

The heart is deceitful above all things and beyond cure.
Who can understand it? — Jeremiah 17:9 (NIV)

The young company commander was hurting.

She was in pain, but not from any physical shrapnel wounds that would put her in the hospital with a Purple Heart pinned to her pillow like many in the Iraqi combat theater.

It was a wound of the heart, the soul, one of betrayal. But the pain was real enough. In fact, a bullet wound from the enemy might be easier to recover from than this one.

It was in essence a friendly fire wound from her own unit, from another American soldier, from a leader she was supposed to trust.

"It hurts, Sir. It really hurts. I feel worse over this than going through the whole war."

Sometimes failure and betrayal are much worse enemies than any ideology or political system we may be in combat against. It was for her a "death," albeit not a physical one. It was the death of idealism, of the way one thought the world and life ought to be, but turns out it wasn't and probably never will be again.

Why is it that life's most important lessons are almost always born at the expense of pain? Perhaps that is why we call them "the hard lessons of life, the school of hard knocks." Like birth, growth is never an easy, painless process; worth it, yes; but, oh, so difficult when we are in the midst of it.

As we age, as we become old chaplains, not much surprises us anymore. We have seen the greatness of human beings and the magnificent overcoming of the worst of life ... and we have seen much more of the worst that Homo sapiens can produce, as well.

On occasion, we are amazed at the heights and depths of humanity, but in order to survive in working with people we, too, have had to temper our idealism and hopes of the way life ought to be with the dreadful reality of the way life often is.

Like Jeremiah, the Lord's prophet of old, we marvel at the depths of human depravity, shake our heads, and can only conclude, "The heart is deceitful above all things and beyond cure. Who can understand it?"

This young West Pointer, an intelligent, good soldier and commander had just experienced the death of her idealism in a bout with the worst characteristic of another human being and the lesson, as all powerful lessons demand, stung her soul badly.

"I feel, Sir," she said "like I've been through a death." And while she will hear no "Taps" or funeral sermon or 21-gun salute, something had died within her and she was feeling the draining effects of loss and grief.

She happened to be a soldier in Iraq, but this could, and does, happen to us anywhere we interact with other fragile, sinful human beings. When dreams die or life's often brutal realities dawn harshly on young, hopeful, idealistic minds and souls, the result can be just as devastating as the death of a loved one.

The issue would sound pretty normal in the interaction between human beings in any occupation. A first sergeant of a company was unwilling to lead by example, she often thwarted and bypassed the commander and when confronted, and she decided that her legacy would be to inflict as much harm as possible on the young commander. Unfounded accusations were hurled and while mud thrown may not stick to a person, it always leaves even the innocent stained.

It is the classic manipulator's ploy. "I will get what I want by any means necessary, and I will get it at whomever's expense it takes. If not, then I will make your life intolerable."

When people of integrity cannot and will not bow to such threats, they must often take the wrath and mudslinging of one who feels completely unbound by any sense of integrity or rules of fairness. "Anything goes" is how they have learned to live their lives with others.

This is what the young commander was up against, and the battle had taken its toll.

The death of reason and good will is the first casualty in idealism's temperance. Most often the young approach the world with an "I trust that your motives are as good as mine are. Let's work together and we can get the job done." But the fact of the matter is that while many people are trustworthy and have good motives, many are not. Wisdom and leadership dictate that all cannot be trusted and caution is warranted.

The feeling of death in this young commander was that she had failed to win over, or failed to come to a trusting working agreement with the top enlisted soldier in her company and that must mean that she failed.

What she needed to know was that she can never control the will of another and that while she can certainly encourage that kind of trusting relationship, she cannot command it. Many are not interested in cooperation, only in their self-aggrandizing agenda no matter how much goodwill one person extends to another.

It is a hard lesson to learn for those of us who would like to go through life believing that there is good in everyone and that, when given the chance, all will take the high road. We'd like to believe that trust rendered will be trust returned and many times this is so.

But not always.

Some people are so self-centered that no amount of trust or kindness will change them when they feel their agenda or desires are threatened.

It is a hard lesson to learn. But it must be learned to one degree or another. The challenge is to recognize that we live in a fallen, sinful world with fallen, badly broken people and yet to not become so skeptical and hardened that we lose all faith in humankind and God's power to renew, remake, and reshape broken vessels into joyful vessels brimming with new life, new wine.

Jesus knew what he was saying when he told his followers so long ago, "... so be wise as serpents and innocent as doves" (Matthew 10:16 NRSV).

Yes, doves hurt, but they can also still take wing and fly into the arms and power of the God who only knows too well the treachery and hatred of people, the very people he came to save.

Sometimes being shot at by the enemy is a far more desirable type of combat than being shot at by one of your own.

Yes, it hurts, Sir.

But a lesson learned now for a dove may preclude a far worse betrayal and pain later from a slithery human serpent.

Change Of Command

The movement is exaggerated and awkward, but fluidity is not the point.

Each soldier steps out of the position of attention with one foot forward and grasps the unit guidon, the unit flag. Then coming back to attention, they pass it to the next person in the diamond formation. Going full circle, the flag reaches the originator in less than a minute as a narrator speaks of the significance of each passing of the flag.

This is the Army's Change Of Command ceremony, which involves great symbolism that reaches beyond the sphere of military life. One commander has finished their time as the leader responsible for everybody and virtually everything that takes place in their military unit. It is an exhausting, but exhilarating time for most officers. It is the bread and butter of their military career. It is as close to being a god as they will ever get in life.

Within legal limits, their word is law and affects every aspect of a soldier's life assigned to that unit. Command Time is one of the great career gates for U.S. Army officers. So, a change of command ceremony is a bittersweet event for officers. There is relief from the constant responsibilities, the midnight emergencies, and long hours of work, but there is also sadness at no longer commanding, leading troops, at being the key to the unit, and of exercising so much power over the lives of so many people.

No matter the elation or sadness of the commander and unit, the Change Of Command ceremony is a time-honored way among soldiers of expressing an altering situation. It is the symbolism that catches the eye of the chaplain. Apart from the normal invocation, this ceremony has no religious connotations, yet the underlying symbols do equate strongly to the realm of the spiritual. The unit is assembled before the commander. The senior NCO, a first sergeant for a company-sized element or a command sergeant major for a battalion or higher unit, carries the symbol of the unit — its flag or guidon.

In times past, the colors of the regiment was the key signal in battle of where to go and who to follow. The task of carrying the colors in battle traditionally fell to the bravest soldier or the color sergeant. Honor dictated that no matter how many flag bearers fell in battle, someone must always pick up the unit flag and carry it forward, never surrendering it to the enemy's grasp. The number of captured enemy colors or the number of unit flags lost measured battles won or lost in the past.

The flag became a powerful symbol of units and soldiers who subordinated their individual identity and will to that of a larger whole. In a modern Army, the flags are not carried into battle. However, they remain potent reminders of identity and loyalty. The command sergeant major is still the keeper of the unit colors. The CSM is opposite the senior commander in the diamond shape, who alone has the power to appoint an officer to command one of their units. Flanking the lone senior enlisted soldier is the outgoing commander and the incoming commander.

Taking the unit flag from the guidon, the CSM and the outgoing commander make the exaggerated movement toward each other, at the same time grasping the staff of the flag. Releasing the flag, the CSM returns to attention while the commander grasps the symbol of authority for the last time. They then execute the same movement, except this time going toward the senior commander. In this symbolic gesture, power is passed to a greater one who then is free to bestow that power on to the next commander.

With the same exaggerated movements, the flag is passed on to the new leader who then returns the flag to the command sergeant major for safekeeping. In less than a minute, the whole procedure is concluded, but real power has symbolically been changed. Soldiers now legitimately take orders only from the new commander, while the old commander shuffles off to a new assignment. It is a short, but effective way of communicating change in a unit.

The old chaplain in me can't help but look upon these movements and symbolism, seeing parallels to the world of the Spirit. A baptism, a conversion, however one may want to label the life-changing event of surrendering one's life to the Savior, Jesus Christ, is in essence a change of command.

Repeatedly the New Testament writers speak of a rebellious humanity, you and me as being transformed enemies of God. Saint Paul explains:

> *(13) God rescued us from dead-end alleys and dark dungeons. God has set us up in the kingdom of the Son God loves so much, (14) the Son who got us out of the pit we were in, got rid of the sins we were doomed to keep repeating. (21) You yourselves are a case study of what God does. At one time, you all had your backs turned to God, thinking rebellious thoughts of him, giving God trouble every chance you got. (22) But now, by giving himself completely at the cross, actually dying for you, Christ brought you over to God's side and put your lives together, whole and holy in God's presence.* — Colossians 1:13-14, 21-22 (The Message)

The change of command from one allegiance to another by faith in Christ has forever changed the equation in our lives. God made the change possible through his Son's death on the cross and Christ's resurrection from the grave. God does it all. Our only alternative is to hold the Change Of Command ceremony. We, as the keeper of our flag — our identity, our will, the power over our hearts that God has allowed each person to hold — is now offered freely, willingly, to the Savior.

In an exaggerated movement or not, in a public ceremony or quietly in a Humvee in Iraq, a soldier, a sinner gives the flag of their souls to the Senior Commander, the Son of God and says in effect with or without eloquence, "Lord, I yield command of my life to you. Take all of me, the good, the bad, and the ugly." Then, taking the flag of surrender with a gentleness and joy that shocks the undeserving sinner, Jesus does a surprising thing. He hands the flag with a smile to the Holy Spirit who then, in joy, hands it back to the sinner who has become son or daughter.

But the flag is different. It is cleansed; it has become pure and new words grace the restored flag: "This is my beloved son ... this is my beloved daughter ... with whom I am well pleased." And without having done one single thing to have earned this change of command, a new son, a new daughter is welcomed by God into God's family.

The Holy Spirit becomes the command sergeant major for the new soldier of Christ. The presence, guidance, and encouragement of the Holy Spirit preserves the flag in the multitude of battles and skirmishes that lay ahead for the Christian. The decisive change has taken place and the one who is in command has promised to bring all soldiers/sons/daughters safely home.

Perhaps the Army can teach us all how to do more than curse efficiently, sleep in the dust, and eat bad food. Maybe its most important lesson is to teach us the importance of a change of command with the Supreme Commander and Savior, Jesus Christ.

Honor: The Final Salute

They came to the center aisle and stopped smartly in front of the memorial display. There stood the time-honored symbols of the military in death: flags, helmet perched on an inverted rifle, and boots placed together as if at the military position of attention.

Beginning with the general, each soldier present advanced to the memorial with the soldier's picture on display, executed a crisp salute, did an about face, and walked out of the tent used as the Camp Anaconda Chapel. Row by row each soldier in desert uniform rendered a final salute to a fallen comrade whose dog tags now hung from the M-16 rifle.

It was a memorial ceremony in Army parlance; a non-religious service for the unit to remember and reflect upon the life of one of their own, a life now gone, a life that must be said good-bye to, one that requires some formal recognition of its absence on earth. Each soldier comes to the accepted symbol of military loss and death: the crossed flags, American and U.S. Army, hanging above the stand holding the rifle with fixed bayonet inverted as if to mark the grave of a soldier on the battlefield. A helmet sits upon the rifle butt with its rank sewn on the camouflage cover indicating that a sergeant has died and those present have come to give their last effort of soldierly respect.

One-by-one they come, some pausing longer than others, some executing their military movement and salutes more crisply than others, but they all come for the one final salute of honor. It matters not how much or how little each soldier knew or remembered the deceased. What matters is that he was a fellow soldier, a comrade in arms, one of their own who died in a foreign land, in a hostile environment and in this combat zone young men and women of the United States military are more aware than ever of the preciousness of human life. So they come to offer the respect universal to all soldiers: one final salute.

The culmination of the ceremony is a gut-wrenching, somber, and touching martial ritual. The eulogies are completed, the chaplain has finished his words of comfort and hope, the music has ceased, and the last roll call begins. Recreating a first formation to account by name for all the soldiers assigned to the company, the first sergeant moves to the front of the chapel, does an about face before the assembled soldiers and announces, "Roll Call!"

Coming to attention, all hear the first sergeant call out a soldier's name. The present soldier responds with a loud and clear "Here, First Sergeant!" Another name, then another, and another; each time the response is the same, "Here, First Sergeant!" Then the deceased soldier's name is called out. Silence. He calls again. Silence. A third time, only louder, as if more volume will reach into the grave. Continued silence. Then from the ranks another soldier responses, "First Sergeant! SGT Jones is no longer with us!"

Those hard words sink in deeply as the first sergeant stands away from the weapon, helmet, boots, and dog tags and the haunting strains of "Taps" flows through the chapel. No muscle moves, not a limb twitches. All are ramrod straight as American soldiers stare straight ahead through eyes that bear reflections, devotion, loss, and respect. The trumpet fades with the last of its melancholy echo and the individual saluting of the military equipment symbolizing life as a soldier begins. It is a touching moment even for those who have seen more death than they want to remember. But death cannot be avoided, only denied, and only to the detriment of the human psyche.

So they come, reflect, and salute one last time. But today's ceremony is different, not in form, but in tone, and that is what makes this ceremony doubly difficult. The soldier did not die from hostile fire, but rather from fire from his own hand. Suicide.

This situation sets off such a firestorm of conflicting thoughts and emotions within us all, but particularly soldiers who have faced the brutal reality of war and survived, only to see one of their own die by his own hand. Death they have come to accept in a degree far more real to them than to most of their peers back home, but death by suicide is so much more difficult to understand, to accept, to rationalize. As in all self-inflicted deaths, the emotions of those left behind, those who must pick up the pieces and put some semblance of order and meaning back into life despite the gaping hole left in their soul and hearts, run from anger to confusion and outright incredulity.

Questions rage, "Could we have seen this coming? Could we have prevented it? Why didn't we realize there was a problem?" The memorial service doesn't end or answer the questions; it merely announces the beginning of the long, hard process of coming to grips with what has happened and the grief that lurks in the long, waking nights. "Why did this soldier think this was the only way out? There is always hope, isn't there? Yes, there had been a dishonorable act, but what about the family left behind? What about us? What honor is there in a death like this?"

Maybe this soldier felt they had no honor and would rather die. "Death Before Dishonor" is a motto lived out by many, particularly in the military. Honor is really what conflicted so many about this ceremony, this last rendering of military honor to be followed by a 21-gun volley at the final committal service. Soldiers, especially in combat, are taught to rely and depend upon their battle buddies, their comrades in the foxhole or fighting vehicle, and when one of them is felled by the enemy, troops have nothing left to offer but their tears, their respect, the giving of their final sign of honor even in death — a salute. The salute says by its very nature, "You, my friend, died for something that matters: comrades, friends, home, freedom, faith, nation. It is an honor to salute you this one last time."

But what does a soldier with a cloud hanging over their head die for? What meaning is there in a death because of dishonorable deeds? Thus the conflict. Does rendering honor to one who commits suicide encourage or tacitly endorse others to exit when life is at its bleakest? Is it still appropriate to offer one's respect based not on the hideously poor choice of their last moments, but on the totality of their lives before this final dark moment? When given a choice, the latter is the most gracious and merciful response appropriate to most soldiers.

"Salute the soldier, not the action!" is the message. Name it wrong, call it what suicide is — a selfish act that stigmatizes the survivors for the rest of their lives — but commend the person to a merciful God whose tears are just as real as any soldier's in that chapel service today. The last soldier salutes, does an about-face and walks out into the gathering heat of the Iraqi summer morning.

A lone figure remains, that of the first sergeant who called out his soldier's name to no response as "Taps" echoed through the unit's soul. Staring ahead, deep in thought, deeply troubled, he rises from his seat and stands again before the memorial display. His desert boots snap together in attention, his arms stiffly at his side just as he was taught in basic training almost two decades ago. A welling tear begins as lips quiver in a final word of goodbye to a friend as the soldier in him struggles to contain the emotions that are determined to flow. The battle subsides and his arms return to his side followed by an about-face that he has executed a thousand times in the Army.

He marches down the chapel aisle. He has many more soldiers he must still feed, care for, and protect. And, by the grace of God, he prays he will never again struggle under these circumstances to render a final salute of honor and to hear the words, "First Sergeant! SGT Jones is no longer with us!"

How Sweet The Sound!

The notes from the instruments were barely heard at the end of the stadium, but yet were instantly recognizable. The sound of the familiar hymn that has come to be a symbol of comfort echoed only loudly enough from the Army band brass quartet to give the mind and soul the faintest hint of what was being played. But it was enough. Only the Lord knows how many of the several hundred soldiers standing and singing "Amazing grace, how sweet the sound!" really knew or believed what they were singing, but it is the melody itself that somehow communicates and comforts the soul in our culture.

From presidents to astronauts to soldiers killed in a vehicle accident, the public farewells to our nation's fallen have almost always included this stately hymn by a repentant English slave trader almost 300 years ago. It has become an accepted cultural expression of loss, even among those outside of the Christian tradition; an expression in which we acknowledge death's presence in the loss of a comrade, friend, or loved one.

The faint notes of "Amazing Grace" drifted on this Iraqi morning to acknowledge the death of a unit commander; not from the hazards of war, but death in Kuwait from a vehicle accident. In what is truly a tragic and cruel irony that this life thrusts upon humans, the commander survived the war in Iraq itself only to lose his life in peace while preparing his unit for that most joyful of military activities — going home after a long and danger-fraught deployment to a combat theater of operations. The place where the brass quartet played "Amazing Grace" was an American base inside Iraq where many Army units that the commander controlled or affected were still deployed for peacetime sustainment operations. A soccer stadium provided the setting for the memorial service where troops sat on dusty cement bleachers in their desert uniforms.

To soldiers with weapons in hand and heavy Kevlar helmets on, the rising Middle Eastern sun gave off more and more heat with each passing minute. A pair of desert boots sat at the base of an anchored M-16 with bayonet that was inverted and pointing downward. On the weapon was a pair of dog tags with silencers topped by a Kevlar helmet. The officer's rank was sewn on the camouflaged cover just above the camouflage headband. A picture of the deceased commander stood at the base of these symbols of a fallen soldier, overshadowed by a U.S. Army flag.

Probably few soldiers there that morning in the Iraqi sun knew the commander in a personal way. When the P.A. system did not function, those too far away to hear the unaided voice learned nothing more of the man's character and life. But in a strange way, that did not seem to matter. All that most soldiers knew was that another soldier had died. They knew the task of those who live: say good-bye, render respect and honor, even when they do not know them personally.

Nurture the living, care for the wounded, honor the dead are the three tasks of the chaplain corps, and soldiers carrying weapons with live rounds in what was a hostile environment understand the need to honor the dead, even those they have never met. But, when words fail or are just garbled sounds mixed among the cacophony of a normal busy Army day, symbol and music reach through to the soul. Better than any sermon or eulogy, the desert boots and helmet suspended on a rifle instantly tell soldiers that one of their own has become a casualty and honor is due. Yet it is the music that strikes most deeply to most.

Though "Amazing Grace" is truly a hopeful hymn of faith for Christians, its slow and stately melody communicates a solemnity that expresses loss and grabs our often wayward and dull souls by the lapels saying, "Wake up! Listen! This is important. This matters!" Just hearing a few notes causes soldiers to bow their heads, and it is not from the load of a heavy helmet, for the necks of these men and women long ago became adjusted to its constant wear. Rather, it is respect — respect for one they did not know, but who was also "one of us, one of our own who now is gone."

Soldiers in the field who eat, sleep, work, and endure together 24 hours a day understand better than their civilian counterparts that you must take care of your own; you must look out for your battle buddy because that is the only way anyone can survive to go home.

We need comrades, we need friends, we need nameless battle buddies to help us, as we help them, through the fog of war and battles and beyond — whether that be in Iraq, in an emergency room in Oregon, or the funeral home in Iowa. We need others, for this life is far too difficult and far too dangerous to be a lone ranger. We American individualists discover in the military that lone rangers are only for the movies. That reality becomes the conviction that no man is an island as John Donne, the English man of faith, wrote centuries ago. We need one another in life and death.

When one of our own falls, even in such ordinary tragic circumstances as a vehicle accident, it still brings us to pause, to remember, to bow our heads in respect. So, heads were bowed for a fallen comrade as they stood and listened, "Amazing grace, how sweet the sound that saved ..." How sweet the sound.... How can this be, even in death's chilling presence? So strange and yet so strangely true. The sound is sweet to our souls only because we know the power behind the words of this converted, repentant slave trader, a power that makes the tune sad to our ears, but strangely wonderful in its powerful hint of triumph.

The bowed heads did not last long. The hymn's conclusion brought more audible words from a chaplain until the band began to play again. This time the sound snapped bowed heads upright and bodies stiffened to attention. "Taps" drifted in the still Iraqi air. Its sound spoke louder than any human voices. Without command, soldiers rendered their respect and honor the best way they knew how while the strains of mournful loss echoed over the stadium as hundreds of American soldiers saluted one of their own for the last time.

Like the words of the hymn, the words of "Taps" are also lost on most of those saluting respectfully. It is a bugle call that signals "death" and "separation" to our soul, but it was never intended as such. According to one authority, this song arose in the Civil War at the command of General Daniel Butterworth. It was a "Lights out" order over the tents of the Union Army of the Potomac with words that do not belie death but rather rest after the day's toil of marching and perhaps battle.

1. Day is done, gone the sun,
From the lake, from the hills, from the sky.
All is well, safely rest, God is nigh.

2. Fading light, dims the sight,
And a star gems the sky, gleaming bright.
From afar, drawing nigh, falls the night.

3. Then good night, peaceful night,
Till the light of the dawn shineth bright,
God is near, do not fear — Friend, good-bye.*
[*author's addition]

Not death, but peace and rest the words bid us to know. It is the knowledge and security of God's gracious presence that gives the tune its power, for a melody without meaning is like a rider without a horse. It is a call — a bugle call for all who hear its sound to believe the words: All is well, safely rest, God is nigh. God is near, do not fear — Friend, good-bye.

The sound is mournful. Its words are hopeful. Is that not what we need to hear on a Memorial Day or at any service where we remember and say good-bye to our friends and loved ones? Any time we acknowledge loss, we must also retain hope. Our hope that God is near, that God does care for us, our loved ones, and our world, despite all the confusing and incomprehensible circumstances that lead to problems, pain, and even death. God's amazing love and grace in Jesus Christ, who experienced, yet defeated, death on that first Easter morning, truly saves us, gives us peace, and brings us safely home.

When life forces us to say good-bye how strange it is to hear no words, but only familiar tunes and to still somehow know deep in your soul that even in death all is well. We can safely rest in God's eternal home and those left behind are secure in God's love, wisdom, and plan. No matter where we find ourselves, we can remember and know that our God is always near. One doesn't have to come to a memorial service in a dusty stadium in Iraq to be reminded of these concepts. In thousands of cemeteries around the nation on Memorial Day, small bands of Americans will hear these haunting melodies and recall the same truths that sustained them in their wars, their battles even as their children, grandchildren, and friends are discovering in our most recent war here.

Names of thousands of American veterans will be read, and most will not be remembered, except by an annually dwindling pool of comrades, family, and friends. The vast majority of those named who have flags placed over their graves, will not have died from combat wounds, but rather from an accident, disease, or old age far away from any war zone. But, their graves are no less significant than those killed in action.

For in their service, no matter how mundane, they were comrades, battle buddies, to a friend, to a unit, to a nation who called on them to serve when they would rather have been at home. They served, and whether they died from enemy action or in a vehicle accident on their way home from Kuwait and Iraq, they deserve the bowed head of fellow soldiers, of a grateful nation at the solemn, but hopeful sound of a bugle call.

They deserve the proud salute of soldiers whom they never knew, the salute that says once more, in life or in death; God is near, do not fear — Friend, good-bye. No words heard, only two powerful melodies, and yet hope is rekindled for the tasks ahead until the day comes when in some quiet, windswept cemetery, our names from the Second Gulf War will be spoken while a small American flag implanted over our grave flaps in the air. Then some young soldier looking forward to the cookout at the lake later, will snap to attention for those he or she never knew and salute smartly at the sound of the bugle.

Without a word, that soldier will have said all that really needs to be said to a fellow soldier, for that will be thanks enough. How sweet the sound! Amazing grace, how sweet the sound that saved! Hear its sound — God is near, do not fear.

Ol' What's His Face?

It was a compliment ... I guess.

It was Thanksgiving Day during wartime, but soldiers had gathered to show their gratitude. The general was on the chancel of the chapel tent giving a greeting to the assembled soldiers. He mentioned something he had heard at a prayer breakfast the week prior as a chaplain talked about thanksgiving.

The commander said, "The chaplain said at this breakfast that there are two things you cannot make someone do. That got my attention," he said. "You cannot make someone love you or make someone grateful if they don't want to be."

Then he mentioned my name, or did he?

Looking at me in the congregation he said, "Chaplain Ettelson is right."

Chaplain who?

He said it again "Chaplain Ettelson." Soldiers looked around. A "Kittleson," but no "Ettelson."

Momentary disappointment flicked across my soul. "Wow, here I am, one of his chaplains whom he sees around most every day and he can't remember my name."

I felt like the proverbial "Ol' what's his face."

Self-pity set in.

"Story of my life: People can't remember my name even in Iraq on a muddy, cool Thanksgiving Day."

There are fewer muddier potholes in life than the one of self-pity. And there are few people who enjoy being around those who are lost in feeling sorry for themselves, even God's Spirit.

So the Spirit spoke quickly and loudly enough for even my dense soul to hear. "So, you're feeling sorry for yourself, eh? So what, if a general doesn't remember your name or mispronounces it? Big deal, Kittleson or Ettelson or whatever your face is called? Your job in life is not to be remembered by others. It is to point them to the Light. Besides, I remember who you are. That is all that matters."

But now, this is what the Lord says ... Fear not, for I
have redeemed you; I have summoned you by name,
you are mine.   — Isaiah 43:1 (NIV)

"Remember, Ettelson: what matters is the message — not you;
the Master, not your name. Isn't that what you said you wanted
when you were called as a servant of God?"

The Spirit then mentioned a fellow named John the Baptist.
"What was his job in the kingdom of God," the Holy One asked,
"to be the light or to bear witness to the light? To point to Jesus or
to point to himself?"

"Lord, you sent John to point to your Son, not to point to himself," I lamely replied.

"Uh-huh. So, if I use you to help others remember something
important on Thanksgiving about their relationship with *me* and
you don't get proper credit for it, are you going to pout and wallow in self-pity or rejoice that you can still be used by me?"

The Spirit's sword, I rediscovered, is still as sharp and double-
edged as the day the pastor of the book of Hebrews first wrote of it
(Hebrews 4:12). It cut to the quick in a hurry.

I wonder how many times in my life and the lives of so many
"servants of God," we seek to be recognized for our labors of pointing to Jesus, the Savior and "Oh, by the way, Lord, please spell
and pronounce my name correctly."

"Lord, I don't need all the credit, but a little wouldn't hurt
either!" We rarely admit those thoughts in public, but often think
them in the deepest recesses of our old Adam-infected souls.

But like John the Baptist, or the little boy with three loaves
and two fish, or the donkey that carried Jesus, the King, coming
into Jerusalem on that first Palm Sunday, or those unnamed disciples encountering the Risen Christ on the road to Emmaus, and
all who have the privilege to point to the Lord of Life and yet are
unnamed, the joy comes in being an instrument of God, of being
useable to accomplish the great and small parts of God's plan.

It is not in having a plaque with our names on it in some forgotten nook or cranny of a church building, but in being an instrument

for the *one* who is life, offers life, and graciously gives life freely as a gift of his love and mercy.

We are the road sign along the highway that no one remembers, which helps the traveler find the way home, unnoticed, unremarkable, yet essential to the journey.

We professionals of the church (pastors, chaplains, men and women of the cloth) ought to know this. But we forget like everyone else. We are human beings with wants, desires, and needs like anyone else and sometimes our desire to serve the Lord may not have the purist of motives. We want our names printed correctly for all to see on the program and in the bulletin. We want people to know our lofty status, our rank (so important in a military culture), our titles and awards. We sometimes forget that the great reversal is that "the first shall be last and the last first" in God's kingdom.

We sometimes forget what our true calling is from our God.

When we do, every once in a while God grabs us by the stacking swivel (a common military saying referring to the a metal device on a weapon that allows soldiers to stack together their weapons in a tripod or other shape) and gets our attention, again.

Sometimes he even uses Army generals. (Imagine that?)

Thanksgiving Day, I had to be reminded once again what my calling is in the kingdom of God. And, in being reminded of that, to recall what is the job of all who belong to God's family through the forgiveness of the crucified and risen Savior; whether pastors or UPS drivers or cookie makers, our lives are to point to the light of the world in whatever way we can, directing all within our influence, not to our names, credentials, or accomplishments, but to the Living Christ as we remember, joyfully, our true mission statement; the mission statement of all baptized believers:

> *In the same way, let your light shine before others, that*
> *they may see your good deeds and praise your Father*
> *in heaven.* — Matthew 5:16 (NIV)
> (Jesus from the Sermon on the Mount)

The message is what counts — not the messenger; the light — not the lamp stand.

This Thanksgiving Day in Iraq, I find myself grateful for all the things that a person should be in life: family, love, and God's salvation, for all those things and more ... plus one more.

I'm grateful that a general (or any parishioner) remembered something (anything?) of what I said in a sermon a week earlier at a prayer breakfast; that in itself is a miracle of no mean proportion.

I'm also very grateful that the general messed up my name.

This unintentional mispronunciation has wonderfully reminded me that being a "What's his face" in life is really okay as long as God remembers me, my family loves me, and as long as my thoughts, words, and actions point in the direction of the Savior, the Master, Jesus. For it is his light that this dark and broken world needs, not mine.

I'm grateful that God can, and apparently is, still very willing to use all the "Ettelsons" and "What's his faces" of this world to do his will and to point others to a wonderfully gracious, forgiving deity. For as long as God uses ordinary, unremarkable, unmemorable people, like me, without forgetting my name, I have something amazing to be thankful for no matter where I may eat turkey and dressing this year, or any year.

Thanks, General, for giving me a gift I would never have dreamed of in Iraq on Thanksgiving.

And thanks, Holy Spirit, for reminding one of your "Ol' What's His Faces" of what really matters in this world.

The light — not the lamp stand, the message of the Master — not the sign along the way.

Meester, Meester

A thought for Thanksgiving ...

Like a swarm of hungry mosquitoes they descend upon the American soldiers climbing out of their Humvees in full battle gear quickly scanning the surroundings for potential danger. They come materializing out of every doorway and nook and cranny of the small, friendly village.

These Iraqi children come and within minutes a chorus of chatter over and over repeat, "Meester, Meester."

Iraqi children, like children around the world wherever GIs are found, have learned the art of communication. Their Middle Eastern pronunciation of "Mister" comes out with a broad smile and an extended hand — first to shake hands, then the hand is rotated so that it is palm up in a universal expression of "Give me, gimme."

The context determines the nature of their request. From convoys the request is food (yes, even MREs) and water bottles. For others, candy, perhaps, and for school renovations and openings, the plea of "Meester, Meester" is followed by "Peencil, peencil" or its equivalent in sign language — a mimicking of writing on paper.

It is hard for American soldiers not to be generous in response to these persistent requests. The villages are so poor by our standards. The children are cute and bright, and besides, most soldiers like children. Who wouldn't want to help in even the smallest of ways? Only a Scrooge, a miser, a cold-hearted tyrant would not want to help.

But ...

But ... after a few hours of this constant buzzing in the ears of "Meester, Meester, gimme, gimme," even the kindest of soldiers' souls tends to lose patience and become hardened. There is absolutely no peace, no let-up from the persistent begging accompanied by the most pitiful expressions formulated on children's faces that would make Hollywood actors blush with humility at their own acting skills compared to these children. After repeated hours of this, soldiers actually volunteer to climb up in the hot-to-the touch Humvee turret to man the .50 cal machine gun even on a sizzling day to get away from the swarm. One even begins to think kindly of Ebenezer Scrooge as the hours, the heat, the weight of the combat gear, and the Kevlar helmet sap one's compassion and patience.

"Meester, Meester ..." is heard so often, in fact, that even after returning to the base, and finally removing the helmet and heavy battle gear, the weary soldiers sink onto the cot, still hearing those echoing words while seeking sleep in another Iraqi night.

"Meester, Meester ..."

Why would these two words, out of all the words spoken in a day, stand out so much?

It dawned upon me the other day, during a village visit, that this must be what it is like for our Heavenly Father when we pray. I pray and what God hears all day long, from me and from millions upon millions of believers, must sound like a swarm of annoying requests.

"Meester God, Meester God! Gimme, gimme!" We may throw in a "Please" or an "In Jesus' name" or an even rarer "If it be your will, Lord," but the basic message is the same — "Lord, give me this, give me that" — like children in a poor Iraqi village.

No one really blames the children in the village for their persistence. They are poor. They have many needs; of that there is no doubt. But, is my prayer life any different than their persistent pleas?

We act as if we have as many needs as the poor of any village, and if we ask long enough and loud enough, that even if it isn't God's will, maybe he'll grant it anyway, just to get us off his back. Physical children on earth and God's spiritual children seem to believe that with a parent or Parent, bug them enough, wear them down enough and they will cave in to the request just out of sheer desire for some peace and quiet.

Jesus even seems to give some credence to this idea in the parable of the persistent widow in Luke 18. Be persistent. Keep asking. Your God will speedily answer.

Our lesson from this passage cannot be that our Heavenly Father should be worn down by our constant nagging, even whining, prayers. No, God delights in his children; he knows and cares about their needs. We know that Jesus tells us to persevere; to never quit seeking what is good, unselfish, and right, then in God's good timing he will answer.

The point is not about God's answering our prayers, but about how many Christians and I pray. I usually don't have a problem praying too much, nor necessarily asking too much of God. The point is that asking, begging, or pleading are the vast majority of my prayers, little else.

"Meester God, Meester God! Gimme, gimme!" Over and over and over again.

I wonder if God doesn't sometimes yearn for his children to simply come and seek to express their love and gratitude despite all the very many deep and great needs they all have in their lives; yearn to hear maybe once in a while, "Thank you, Lord," more than "I want, Lord."

I wonder if God doesn't yearn for his redeemed children, his beloved family through the sacrifice of his Son, to have a conversation with him of praise and thanksgiving rather than being swamped with whining, begging, or even demanding that God do this, give that?

When is the last time we talked to God and said, "Lord, I don't need a thing today. I just wanted to tell you, 'Thanks.' Thank you for your Son, for life, for my family, my comrades, for a nation and all you've done for me and for those I love"?

To my great chagrin, I don't recall one time recently when I told my Heavenly Father that without at least throwing in one or two or more "Oh, by the way, Lord, please gimme...."

Maybe that is why Thanksgiving is still important for us as Americans. It is not, of course, a religious holiday in our country. It is a national day to give thanks. This is a great idea no doubt, but not one tied to any church calendar.

The day has, in fact, lost much of its meaning as turkey, football, and family get-togethers (all good things) have become the focus of a day where both the turkeys and the humans get stuffed. A secular society sees little need to thank any deity, but is more importantly possessing a school break or a four-day weekend. The rendering of thanks to God is far down on the priority list, if on the list at all.

Perhaps this year, we as individual Americans can begin to reclaim the holiday, by first remembering the original meaning of the word "holiday" was "a holy day," a holi-day of gratitude, of thanksgiving.

And the best way to begin reclaiming the day for ourselves and our culture is to stop and think of our blessings so we can pray with gratitude.

There is some evidence that the Anglo-Saxon root word for "thankfulness" is "think-fulness." Thanksgiving first should be a holiday full of thinking, for without this aspect we only see our needs and wants, focusing only on ourselves and not lifting our eyes to the source of our life and blessing.

In doing so, perhaps, this Thanksgiving can become the one holy day of our year where we abandon all our persistent patterns of "Gimme, gimme. Amen" petitions. Perhaps we could abandon them for just one day and instead of a perfunctory, obligatory Thanksgiving meal table prayer by the youngest member of the clan seated at a card table in the living room with all the other children, while the adults sit at the main table filled with more magnificent food than a battalion of hungry troops could possibly eat in a week, we will stop, think, and then simply pray an unre-hearsed, heartfelt prayer that surely will bring a smile to our blessed Heavenly King. A prayer lifted not just to bless the turkey, stuffing, or pumpkin pie, but a simple, high and holy prayer to our loving and gracious God. A prayer like:

"Meester God, Meester God! Thank you, thank you!"

For even if we return to our self-absorbed ways the day after Thanksgiving as we battle other Christmas shoppers in the first great assault of the shopping "do-or-die" season, at least we will have had one day where we never asked a thing of God, showing just plain, old-fashioned, unadulterated gratitude.

Many a soldier in this hostile fire zone called Kuwait/Iraq will stop and definitely think about this holiday season as they have perhaps never done before. Most of what is familiar to them is gone this year. No four-day weekends to get away, no family get-togethers to drive to, no snow or football to watch, no family to argue with or draw names out of a hat for Christmas presents. There will be just more soldiering, more duty, sometimes more danger.

They, along with their families back home, will eat their Thanksgiving meal this year with lonely, but also grateful thoughts of home, their loved ones, their nation, and their comrades in arms here and around the globe. Those far from home in the midst of danger tend to stop more, think more, and almost always recall their blessings and what matters most in life.

These soldiers who have stopped to think will be surrounded by large numbers of others in desert camouflage savoring their holiday meal of turkey and all the trimmings, quietly bowing their heads as they do at every meal whether in the chow hall or over an MRE while on patrol, or in a convoy preparing to barrel down an Iraqi highway and on this holi-day will mumble a prayer never more sincere and heartfelt than on this day, a prayer not just thankful for food, but one of gratitude for life, loved ones, freedom, and peace as they simply pray: "Meester God, Meester God ... Thank you! Thank you!"

Saint SGT Murphy

A thought for All Saints' Sunday ...

He was a big, African-American soldier with an obviously Irish name; a chaplain's assistant, a buck sergeant. I was so happy to see him I could have kissed him.

SGT Murphy was a fixture at the chapel in Camp Virginia, Kuwait, prior to the war in Iraq's beginning. He and his infantry unit were assigned to guard the base camp that housed the corps headquarters and the brains of all of the Army's combat forces, should the order come to cross the berm and destroy Saddam Hussein's army.

Right across from the nerve center of the corps headquarters was the camp's chapel tent, a white become tan color from daily wind and dust storms. Every morning inside that tent lined with a pattern image of a mosque in bright yellow, SGT Murphy would gather with a half dozen of his brothers in the faith and pray. Infantrymen, combat soldiers standing in a circle, unashamedly holding hands in unity, talking with the Supreme Commander-in-Chief of the Universe.

As the camp chaplain, I would come to prepare for the devotions that were part of the daily worship ritual there in the desert, and almost always there would be SGT Murphy with his group of warriors.

They were praying, mostly for others, usually for those suffering or waiting in anxiety back home, or for fellow soldiers struggling with problems even as they prepared for battle. After all those prayers were spoken only occasionally would a heaven-bound petition be thrown in for their own safety as the build up for war became frighteningly evident. SGT Murphy was a big man, not a giant, but just a big man physically. But in my mind he was a giant of a man in the things of God and the Spirit. If he had wanted to be "lean, mean, and socially unacceptable" as infantrymen like to portray their image, he could have done so easily and would have been a formidable force.

But he wasn't that way at all. He was as gentle, caring, and as kind as a man could be. He'd shake everyone's hand no matter where he saw you, and that was quite a task considering the vast sea of soldiers chowing down in the heat of the stifling mess tent while wearing full battle rattle (combat gear). He'd readily greet all, salute, if needed, but always be swift to wave or greet, even as troops trudged with their heads down and scarves up protecting against the wind-borne, biting desert sand.

His gentleness made even the most reluctant of strangers feel welcome and safe. You just couldn't help but like him as he assisted his chaplain at Camp Virginia through SCUD drills and combat training.

But one day in mid-March, SGT Murphy and his group were not at the chapel to pray nor did they return to the chapel or to the camp. They had been ordered north to assembly areas awaiting the final order to go to war.

It isn't just the families left behind that sit in anxiousness and uncertainty about soldiers in war. Many a fellow soldier who supported the front line troops from Kuwait, also sat and wondered how their friends and comrades were faring 100 miles north. They, too, listened to the combat reports, took infrequent opportunities to gather in any information, any rumor from other soldiers who were in-the-know or even from know-it-all television analysts from FOX or CNN, always standing before the monitor with helmet in hand and combat and chemical gear hanging from weary, dust-choked bodies. Like back home, it was still difficult to get any news, much less accurate information. Sometimes, we cringed when we did hear news that brought war home to reality.

The maintenance unit that was ambushed with seven killed, the now-famous rescued PFC Jessica Lynch, the soldiers killed in ones and twos whose names came across the news ticker on the television news were people with whom we had probably stood in line at the chow tent or the PX or the phone tent. But for six weeks we heard nothing of SGT Murphy or his chaplain or his unit except that one of their number had been killed in action. Many times in life, prayer is all we can do for one another. There was no lack of that.

One day in early May, he walked into the chapel tent and I have rarely shaken a hand so readily, so gratefully. SGT Murphy had come through the fight alive, exhausted like all, but they had made it and he had returned to his familiar "haunt" — the chapel tent. It was so good to see him. It dawned upon me in reflecting on the joy of seeing this soldier, whom I had known so briefly, that SGT Murphy was a metaphor of the life of faith, as well as being a gentle, spiritual giant.

I imagine our final day on earth and our entry into the kingdom of heaven, not as one of trying to convince Saint Peter to open the gates to let us enter, but rather as the people of God who have gone before us, seeing our entry into God's presence and rushing to greet us, shaking our hand, giving us a hug, a kiss of joy, so glad and so grateful that the Savior has brought us through "the fight" and safely home. Like seeing SGT Murphy alive, well, and smiling in that tent in Kuwait will we be greeted with joy and celebration that our Lord Jesus, by his forgiveness and mighty power, has brought us safely through the battle into his gentle, peaceable kingdom? I think so. I hope so.

The Christian celebration of All Saints' Day will now ever include this wonderful image of SGT Murphy in my mind and soul; a buck sergeant, not a colonel or three-star general. No longer will my image be one of stuffy, distant plaster saints of glorious battles and miracles of long ago nor of halos and transfigured purity and stained-glass piety that makes saints seem so remote, so unapproachable, so unlike me and all who are ordinary strugglers in the faith.

The saints I now see are the SGT Murphys of the world, flesh and blood, ordinary men and women of faith doing their best, holding tenaciously on to God's love and presence wherever they find themselves; seeking quietly, humbly, to honor the Savior who has given them life and hope through his death and resurrection; humble people who are no strangers to life's serene joys or its hellaciousness as the powers of darkness assault every human being, sooner, rather than later. They are the unacknowledged foot soldiers of God, entering into humanity's most tragic moments without thought of glory or saintly recognition, doing so simply for love of God, love of others, seeking to honor the one who gave them life by his blood.

Saints like SGT Murphy are all around us. They are ordinary people of faith who would blanch and blush at being labeled a "saint," but whose battles with life's challenges, trials, and tragedies make mortal combat with bullets and bombs seem like a Sunday afternoon picnic.

They are the ones who struggle with grace day after day against injustice or poverty or disease; they are the ones battling wasting diseases, debilitating injuries, and limiting defects and yet still have a graciousness and joy about them, a calmness about life that puts us healthy and whining saints to shame; they are the quiet ones laboring month in and month out in nursing homes or living with autistic children, or seeking to help the addicted recover for just one more day. They are the saints who have been assaulted by life's normal fears and also its worst terrors, yet find it possible to somehow smile, to encourage others to faith, and to thank God for life, even the pain of it. They do it without much applause on this earth, but never without the applause of heaven (as author Max Lucado puts it) that one day they shall hear in all its glorious fullness.

C. S. Lewis told once of sitting in a worship service listening to the music. He considered the church's hymns to be sixth rate music at best and was feeling smugly superior to it all until he looked across the aisle at an elderly man in laborer's clothing, wearing soiled, cheap rubber boots. This humble man was singing the hymn in a deep and earnest faith and with a serenity that shocked Lewis. Looking at this man of faith, Lewis concluded that he, himself, was not even worthy to sit in the same church with that old faithful saint of God.

When the church annually celebrates the faithful heroes of old on All Saints' Sunday and sings that glorious hymn "For All The Saints," look up from your hymnal for a few moments and hopefully without staring too obviously, gaze upon the real, live, but very ordinary saints of God before you. Look at those familiar and not so familiar faces gathered around the Word of God, the bread and the wine and the sixth-rate music; gaze at those saints with battle-worn, arthritic hands, and drooping shoulders who have borne the battle of life and faith for so long, but whose souls are yet vividly alive and well before their Lord; identify those souls of all ages surrounding you who are bearing loads of sorrow, grief, and pain that could sink a battleship or bring the roughest and toughest infantry soldier to their knees in surrender. Then, listen to these spirit warriors sing humbly, joyfully, and somehow through their tears those familiar words of the hymn knowing full well that every "their" means "my."

> *You were* their *Rock,* their *fortress and* their *might ...*
> *You, Lord,* their *captain in the well-fought fight ...*
> *You in the darkness drear,* their *one true light,*
> *Alleluia, Alleluia!* — verse 2

In seeing these saints of God, may we all realize as C. S. Lewis did, that we are not worthy to even be in the same room with those ordinary, but faithful saints of God, except for the graciousness of Jesus Christ, their Captain and our "Captain in the well-fought fight."

No ... SGT Murphy didn't get kissed that day, but the applause of heaven must have been thunderous, and I for one couldn't have been happier or more humbled to see a brother in Christ alive and well and to humbly again shake the big hand of a gentle, genuine, battle-tested saint of God.

So, I have my Saint SGT Murphy.

Who is yours?

Tape-delayed Advent?

I never have cared much for tape-delayed broadcasts.

These are the live events, usually of sports games, on television that have already been played hours or even days before, but have been delayed in broadcasting for one reason or another.

But, every once in a while I bend my principles to these delayed showings especially when it is a college football game and I am 7,000 miles away in the Middle East.

Normally, I don't care for these broadcasts because the final score is already well known. It takes a hardy discipline to not peek or listen to others talk about the game when your intention is to watch it later. How does one *not* listen when someone several feet away says "Did you hear about the game. Wow!" Few sports fans have that kind of iron will to plug their ears.

In many respects, watching a game and knowing the final result is akin to reading a mystery novel, but skipping from the beginning to the final chapter. Not being able to stand the suspense of all the in-between chapters, some people will eliminate that suspense by peeking at the ending, or they will say to others "You know how this ends! What happens?"

"Sorry, you'll just have to watch. No suspense. No fun."

Of course, all of the excitement and anticipation is gone when someone gives in and tells us the ending, but neither do people have a coronary because of the suspense, either. I suppose there are trade-offs in life.

Why, then, watch a taped-delayed game unless you are absolutely a true-blue sports fanatic who just can't stand to live without seeing every last second of every game possible?

Well, fans will be fans no matter where they find themselves, whether in Iraq or elsewhere. Viking, Packer, and Big Ten fans all inhabit the military, and many are so committed that they will combat all the different time zones and conditions staying up until the wee hours of the morning just to watch their favorite teams.

Alas, there is a problem here.

Satellite dishes are available, but not plentiful here, and when they are, they aren't always working. So soldiers can watch the

Armed Forces Network (AFN) which carries games live on their channel, but unlike back in the States, there are fewer channels available. When it comes to a big college football Saturday when there are a host of important and rivalry games, choices have to be made. Only a limited number can be broadcast live. The rest, if they are carried at all, must be replayed hours later on a tape-delayed basis.

A Saturday Iowa-Wisconsin college football game was a case in point. It wasn't carried live on AFN because a more important game determining the Big Ten championship was rightly chosen instead. The Iowa-Wisconsin game was shown in a tape-delayed broadcast the next day, on Sunday afternoon.

Military intelligence may not be able to find Saddam, but when it comes to truly essential information like who won the Iowa-Wisconsin football game, nothing is spared to find out the result, and no obstacle to the "intel" is too big.

The proverbial grapevine swings into high gear especially when an Army Reserve unit from Iowa resides nearby. So it was just about impossible to *not know* that Iowa had, in fact, won the game by six points. And, the word was that the game with those Wisconsin cheeseheads was a real "barn burner."

I have to confess that I was elated and relieved to know the result, but I still found myself wanting to see this game anyway, even knowing how it turned out.

It felt like one of those "whodunit" murder-mystery movies where you see right in the opening scenes that a person was done in, but you are left wondering who, how, and why. Then the rest of the movie shows flashbacks, and how bits and pieces of information and interaction all add up to the final result that you already know. The fun of the movie is in seeing the mystery unraveled, how all the pieces fit together, how the plots, twists, and turns of each piece reveals information, and yet knowing the ending doesn't spoil the fun or suspense. Your brain, of course, has to work a little harder this way, but sometimes when you aren't vegetating, that is the fun of the entertainment. Why else watch a mystery?

Such is the case with this football game on tape delay. The mystery is not in the final score, but in the details of each play of the game.

Having read on the internet the game's summary, which team scored what in each quarter, and reading a little of the sequence of the game, I knew not only who won, but how it came about.

Watching the tape-delayed details a day later was just the icing on the cake of knowing how the final score was achieved.

I found myself in front of the tube thinking, "Okay, I know they scored in the second quarter, but there are only two minutes left on this broadcast and Wisconsin even has the ball, so Iowa *has* to score before halftime. That's what ESPN wrote on the internet. So if Wisconsin has the ball with a first down now, there must be a pass interception coming very soon. Iowa has to score."

Voila!

The next play in the broadcast, an interception, was thrown by Wisconsin and the next play after that, Iowa scored. The reporter hadn't invented a fictitious story. He had correctly reported the game.

I followed the rest of the game just that way. Knowing the score by each quarter, I knew that Iowa scored twice in the second half and Wisconsin didn't.

(This, by the way, is a very helpful tool when the need to relieve oneself strikes without pity during the game. "Facilities" are not conveniently located down the hall for soldiers. One must normally hustle outside, sometimes a good forty to fifty meters to find them and hope they aren't all occupied. So, knowing roughly when scoring takes place enables the trooper to dash outside, take care of business, and rush back at a time when the least amount of action takes place. Very useful. After all, how many times has a sports lover even in one's stateside house with a bathroom within a few feet felt a "this-ain't-gonna-wait-no-longer" urge only to have a fabulous play take place while they experience blessed relief? Those remaining watchers of the game hoot and holler over this glorious play to the great chagrin of the one in the facility! Surely it is tragic to the max, but it would have been worse if not for instant replay.)

But ESPN reported that Iowa was only assured a victory on the very last play of the game as Wisconsin had a pass batted down in the end zone.

Whew! That's close, if you're an Iowa fan. "Gotta see that." Sure enough, it was a real barn-burner, worth seeing and watching, even on tape delay.

Having said all that, I wonder if the season of Advent isn't more than a little like a tape-delayed broadcast?

We know the final result.

"Emmanuel — God with us" has come once and he has promised to come again. We remember in the Christmas season how God came long ago in Bethlehem, but in the season of Advent we also look forward in anticipation to God's coming again to set the world right, finally and forever.

We know the end result. Jesus returns triumphantly.

There is a story of a group of seminary students playing basketball at the school's gym which was being cleaned by the old janitor. Being a little taken in by their new-found graduate learning, they asked the janitor if he knew what the book of Revelation meant with all of its cryptic symbolism. He said he did. They smiled a little too proudly at this humble, uneducated janitor as they then asked him, "Really? Okay, what does the book of Revelation mean?"

He quietly replied, "It means Jesus is gonna win."

That's what knowing the score before the tape-delayed broadcast tells us as well.

Yet Jesus, as we live all the in-between chapters of life's story, gives us only vague, generic details of how it all fits together. From the very start we see how the world's "movie" ends up. Now we just have to stick around to see all the details of it being accomplished. We don't need to know all the details ahead of time, just be aware that they point us to the end.

Jesus, though, and the scriptures spend precious little time on all the fine in-between details of the final story. There are some, but not many.

The Lord does make certain, however, that we know the final result: God in Christ has defeated the enemies of evil, sin, and the powers of darkness and will one day finalize the victory by bringing all his faithful people safely home.

By faith, this is our hope as Christians. The rest of our life is lived as a tape-delayed play-by-play, blow-by-blow description of how our Savior went about accomplishing the final victory, in, through, and sometimes despite us.

There may be some barn-burner finishes, close calls and shaves; times when we feel we cannot bear the suspense or struggle any longer, times when we want to quit, times when we doubt that the end result could possibly be true, what the Risen Savior has promised us.

What keeps us in the game is that God will produce that already guaranteed final score, and by the love of Christ and God's amazing grace, we will be on the winning side.

So the next time you hear of a tape delayed broadcast of a great game, don't necessarily hit the remote for something else to watch. Like the Advent season, let this tape-delayed program remind you of all the details of a loving God who already knows the ending of our game and knows we are gonna win in his Son.

Kick back before your spiritual tube and watch all the ins and outs of the struggles, troubles, and hardships in our journey home and then marvel at how God in his love brings it all together making our final score, our ending good. Very, very good.

So who cares if it is a real barn-burner, as long as the right team wins?

"Jesus is gonna win!" whether live or on tape delay.

Probably

Dear Soldier,
 I'm sorry you can't see your family. They prob-ably *miss you very much ...*

So much can hinge on a single word.

The school child's scrawl was on lined paper posted outside out the dining facility. A plywood awning constructed by the engineers protects against the brutal Iraqi summer sun and gives a little, though not much, protection against the wind and dust that accompanies it. Those in Iraq not long after the major combat fighting was done can remember the start of the mess hall and the long, long lines that gathered at every meal as just one facility was open to feed thousands of troops. The long waits in the hot sun made the construction of this modicum of protection a real blessing.

Today, the lines are much shorter as other DFACs (dining facilities) are open and the burden is not all on one facility. But depending upon what time a person goes to chow, a wait is still normal, although not usually a brutal one.

The plywood tunnel-like shelter makes for a perfect place to tack up announcements and notices; important stuff like: "Holiday 5K Run," "Tae Kwan Do Class — Spend Your Time In Iraq Learning How To Kick (Posterier)," "Chapel Holiday Schedule," "Don't Handle Unexploded Ordnance," "Christmas Day Menu," and so on.

Reading the signs helps to pass the time while standing with comrades you've come to eat with almost every day for the last ten months, and apart from complaining about the Army, the list of undiscussed topics is mighty thin.

Someone at DFAC #1 put up a few of the hundreds of letters and greetings from family and friends back home, but especially from children. Most are pretty standard, but we all appreciate the thought, emotion, and effort of American children writing to an unknown soldier in a strange part of the world, a task that is beyond their grasp apart from images of a Rambo or Chuck Norris shoot-'em-up Hollywood movie.

But every once in a while, one grabs your attention. It could be because it reminds you of your children or grandchildren or it may be a phrase, a sentence, or even a word.

In this case, it was a word, the word "probably."

I couldn't help but laugh when I read it the first time. "I'm sorry you can't see your family. They *probably* miss you very much ..."

Do they or don't they?

"Probably" is an adverb that denotes likelihood, but not certainty. "It is very likely that your family misses you, but maybe they don't," the young school child could have written. We all know what they meant, but there is a distinct possibility that not everyone will be missed much, if at all.

After hearing the pitiable stories of so many soldiers as a chaplain, I know that "probably" is a much better word to use than "certainly."

Soldiers mirror society in fractured, dysfunctional families and that mirroring becomes more clouded by the separation, the deployments, the uncertainties of an Army in a sustained and protracted war, the global war on terror, or GWOT, as it is abbreviated. As chaplains are prodded to say in reunion briefings for those near to returning home, "If you had a bad relationship before you left for Iraq, don't expect it to be solved when you get back. After the honeymoon period is over, you'll still have to deal with all the troubles of your relationship, for better or worse."

For those of us so blessed to be in families where there is no "probably," these innocent words of a child give us some humor in what are generally humor-challenged days in Iraq.

For those who are not sure if their loved ones or families do, in fact, miss them, or those who have no one waiting for them to come home, this word of likelihood can be wrenchingly painful.

As a chaplain and pastor, I also can't help but apply this thought to God and his relationship with us, a humanity very much in a troubled relationship with the divine.

What if Jesus announced, "Dear World, I'm sorry you are separated from the Heavenly Father. He *probably* loves and misses you very much."

Well ... does he or doesn't he? Do I have to struggle through life and enter into death some day uncertain and hoping against hope that God does, in fact, love me, forgives me, has a place for me with him in eternity? This would be an existence where I just could never be sure, wondering as the actor did in the old hair coloring commercial touting the natural look of their product, "Maybe she does, maybe she doesn't."

"Maybe God love us, maybe he doesn't? There is a strong likelihood, but no certainty" ... is *not* the message of Jesus, the Christian faith, or of the witnesses of the New Testament.

In fact, the message of Christmas (and the rest of the year) is that the Good News of Jesus Christ announces that God certainly *does* love us. "Make no mistake about it," the gospel proclaims, "we *are* missed. We *are* loved. God *wants* us back in his family. He wants us back so much that he will go to any length to make it a reality. He'll even send his beloved Son to be born as one of us, to grow up to look a fallen world in the eye, and proclaim even while hanging on a brutal cross that there is no "probably" about it. It is a certainty. God, for God-only-knows what reason, loves us absolutely."

> *The angel said to the Bethlehem shepherds, "Don't be afraid. I'm here to announce a great and joyful event that is meant for everybody, worldwide: A Savior has just been born in David's town, a Savior who is Messiah and Master. This is what you're to look for: a baby wrapped in a blanket and lying in a manger."*
> — Luke 2:10-12 (The Message)

> *[Jesus speaking to Nicodemus] This is how much God loved the world: He gave his Son, his one and only Son. And this is why: so that no one need be destroyed; by believing in him, anyone can have a whole and lasting life.* — John 3:16 (The Message)

No probably about it; "Anyone can have ... life," said Jesus.

A story that has always meant much to me is that of a schoolteacher whose extra duties included teaching ailing children to help them keep up with their learning while in the hospital.

One day she was called in to visit a boy who had been horribly burned. The nurses warned her as she was about to enter the room that they were really worried about his survival. He wasn't responding well and seemed to have given up. When she entered the room she was shocked at how badly the boy had been burned and fought the temptation to run from the room herself.

Composing herself, she announced that she was the teacher assigned to help him and proceeded to give him an English lesson on verbs and adverbs. She left after a while, feeling hopelessly inadequate for the needs of this boy.

The next day she dutifully dragged herself to the hospital dreading the pitiful sight of his pain. A nurse saw her and abruptly stopped her saying, "What in the world did you say to that child yesterday?"

Taken aback, the teacher, fearing she had made a bad situation worse, started to apologize, when the nurse shocked her by saying, "Don't apologize. Something happened yesterday after your visit. His whole attitude has changed and he is a transformed person with a will to live like we have never seen in him! Whatever you said, it has changed him."

Confused, the teacher entered into the room, immediately seeing the difference in the boy. Having no idea what she had done, she asked what had happened.

In a simple and profound logic, the burned child said that after her visit yesterday, he thought, "They never would have sent someone to teach me about verbs and adverbs, if they thought I was probably going to die."

No, they wouldn't.

Would God have sent his Son to a hopeless world with little or no possibility of hope, of healing, of redemption?

If we weren't *absolutely* missed, would God have sent his Son to Bethlehem, to Galilee, to the cross and out of an empty tomb? Would he have sent Jesus, the light of life, to a dark and hurting world, into aching, ailing lives, if he didn't *absolutely* love us, *absolutely* miss us, and *absolutely* want us back in his family now and forever and could do something about it?

Probably not.

No ... *certainly not!*

But he has come, this "Emmanuel — God with us," this Jesus whose name means "God saves," and not "God probably saves."

In Jesus Christ, those who have received the gift of being a child of God (John 1:12) have the certainty of God's iron-clad promise: They *are* loved, *are* forgiven, and *are* one of God's own children.

I suspect that most of us *are* probably deeply missed by our families and loved ones, maybe even a friend or two; that we *are* missed with a probability bordering on absolute certainty. But whatever the case, God can use a teacher in a hospital talking about verbs and adverbs, or the scrawl of a child's letter to an anonymous soldier in Iraq standing in line for some good ol' Army chow to remind us that when it comes to his love, there is no *probably* about it.

Martin Luther was fond of reminding parents and children in his catechism of the essentials of the Christian faith, that with God there is no *probably*. He wrote at the end of each section what would become a catch phrase over the centuries for Lutheran Christians who struggled as teenagers to memorize his explanations on the Lord's Prayer, Apostles' Creed, or other prayers. But no matter how hard or long the phrases to be memorized, they could always get the phrase correct that would end each statement, "This is most certainly true."

Not *probably*, but *most certainly* true. It is still a good phrase to remember today.

Yes, God our Heavenly Father *absolutely* loves us, misses us, wants us back, and will go to any lengths to see this come to pass.

"This is most certainly true" for verbs and adverbs and a schoolchild's Christmas letter to a soldier tell us so.

Thanks be to God for when it comes to his love for us, there is no *probably* about it.

Star Of Peace

(This story was written for and appeared in *The Lutheran*, December 2003.)

In Iraq, it shines on soldiers in flak vests and Kevlar helmets.

> *Then the star appeared again, the same star [the Magi] had seen in the eastern skies. It led them on until it hovered over the place of the child. They could hardly contain themselves: They were in the right place! They had arrived at the right time!*
> — Matthew 2:9-10 (The Message)

I've seen more of the stars this last year than ever — in the night skies of Kuwait and Iraq. One can't help but see them here in the desert. In this grand display, one star stands out. We know it isn't really a star but the planet Mars. It's as close to Earth, they say, as it will be for another 63,000 years or so. One wouldn't normally connect Mars and the Star of Bethlehem. After all, Mars is the ancient god of war from which comes such words as "martial." War and the quiet humility of the birth of the Prince of Peace seem 63,000 light years apart.

A poor comprehension of astronomy comes in handy for soldiers at Christmas. With a little imagination, we can easily imagine that bright red star in the sky as the Star of Bethlehem with its polar opposite message of redemption and peace for all. Soldiers and their families have seen the "star of war" far too closely, and they desire, like the Magi, to see and follow the star to the Child who alone brings peace and hope.

This Christmas in our imaginations there will not be just Magi and shepherds kneeling in adoration at the newborn's manger. Soldiers will be there as well, kneeling in a new earnestness before the Child of Peace, for they know and bear the cost of battle. Mortars, bombings, and ambushes are daily realities here in Iraq. Peace is no quaint pie-in-the-sky notion. That longing is even stronger since our extension to a full year of combat duty.

181

Rarely do we hear of fear in the Christmas story. On a closer look, it appears quite often, just as it does in the Easter story. Almost every time it appears, God's messengers tell humanity: "Fear not. Don't be afraid. God is doing something so wonderful, so amazing, that you will hardly believe it." And most of the time they didn't believe it. But that didn't stop God's star from pointing the way to Jesus. Soldiers in this unstable country at Christmas aren't in constant fear. But danger is ever present, making everyone more aware of life's precariousness and preciousness.

During the initial days of the war, a young soldier said to me: "Chaplain, I just got back from combat in Iraq and I'm returning tomorrow. Tell me, please ... what is Christianity all about? I want to know before I go back to the fighting." "It's the story of God's stubborn, amazing love," I quietly said, "that he wants us back in his family so desperately that he came as a child in Bethlehem, lived among us, died for us, and rose from the dead so forgiveness could be ours and we will never again be afraid of life without our loving Savior. It is all a gift for us from Jesus Christ."

He thanked me and said he'd return the next day if his unit had not moved out. He wanted to tell me what he had decided about receiving this gift from God. I never saw him again. Neither did I see his name on any casualty lists.

Yet Christ's love was so near in those precious moments that I'm confident this Christmas in some tent, in a small dusty chapel, on midnight Christmas Eve patrol or on perimeter tower duty somewhere in war-torn Iraq, that young soldier will have followed "the star" to kneel before the Prince of Peace, and he is experiencing the peace of God that passes all understanding. As he kneels with his weapon slung over his shoulder in humble adoration, along with countless other troops spread over this ancient biblical nation — even as they combat not just the enemy but their loneliness and longing for home and family — it won't matter much that the brightest star in the night sky is the "god of war." For the star that matters most — the Star of Bethlehem — shines on bodies and souls in desert camouflage covered by flak vests, Kevlar helmets, and grace.

This Christmas Eve, while traveling to beautiful sanctuaries in peaceful lands for candlelight services, don't forget to look at the brightest star you can see, even if it is the red planet. Then ask your pastor to recall plainly, simply "What this Christianity is all about" so together with brothers and sisters in Iraq and Kuwait we may all kneel before the Prince of Peace, Emmanuel, and know his peace amid all the fears, ambushes, and uncertainties of this broken world. Then, wherever we may be, we know that God's star of peace in Christ Jesus will always be in the right place and at the right time just as the Magi discovered — from kneeling, worshiping soldiers in war to all who would kneel in his peaceful, redeeming love.

Eli's Christmas Tree
(Or Someone In Iowa Loves You)

Is it possible to love someone you have never met or never seen?

I sit here in another Iraqi morning staring at a Christmas tree. It's plastic, twelve inches high; a gift from a generous soul in the States trying to send some Christmas cheer to soldiers far away from home in the Middle East. It will be the first, and hopefully the last, Iraqi Christmas for us.

I tried to add some Christmas lights to it, another gift from a stateside box, but the tree with its wire and green pine needles is far too light to bear the weight, resulting in constant rollovers. I gave up trying to keep the ship upright and decided that the aggravation was probably more than my blood pressure medication could compensate for.

Now my fake Iraqi Christmas tree stands lightless in the windowsill, silhouetted against the designer Army garbage bags that serve as curtains for my office/living quarters. It stands over pictures of my family woven into monthly calendars I've labeled "redeployment" calendars, counting down the months until at least in theory we are to come home after a full year in this hostile fire zone. Pictures of my wife in an herb garden, my son high in the mountains of the Cascades and the Alaskan panhandle, and my daughter with her grandparents posed before Montana mountains at her college graduation taken about the time we pulled into Iraq from Kuwait line up just below the windowsill.

There is only one true ornament on this tree. It is from my mother and one of those gifts that only moms and grandmothers seem to find and buy. It is a ceramic cut-out of the state of Iowa with flowers bordering the saying: "Someone in Iowa loves you." That is the tree's one Christmas ornament, which when compared to most Christmas trees, seems pathetic and pitiful. The scarcity of decorations seems to beg the question, "What use is this tree anyway?"

As it turns out, it is not the quantity that endears this tree to me in this lonely Christmas season. It is its quality. This may be one of my favorite Christmas trees ever, not for its fine craftsmanship, beauty, and exquisite quality, but from what I see in its branches.

My January "redeployment" calendar taped dead-center below the Christmas tree displays my first grandson being held by his mother, father, and his grandmother. His sleeping head covered in a blue knit cap is being lovingly looked down upon by all.

Eli Heeter has entered into this world somewhat reluctantly and late, but to parents and family that love him, that hardly matters now. This child is loved already, not because of what he offers or can do for the family, but simply because of who he is, because others outside of himself have chosen to love him. It is such a gift to enter into this world loved. Many don't ever know that wonder. It is so much like God's undeserved love for us, something we in the faith and church have for 2,000 years called "grace."

Sitting here mulling thoughts for tomorrow's sermon to soldiers at our base in Iraq, and also pondering the deep, imponderable ways of the U.S. Army, I find myself instinctively placing a 2x3-inch picture of my new grandson in the branches of this tree. It had been on the table I use as a desk that is continually covered up by notes or books or coffee cups. I feared it being inadvertently scooped up and finding its way to the garbage bag.

Eli's picture nestles very nicely in the fake greenery of the lower branches, offering me a wonderful view of the newborn from my chaplain/pastor's normal sermon preparation pondering position.

Looking back at me from the picture are two fresh, bright eyes of a little child of God all wrapped up in a towel after one of his first baths in this world. The baby towel is configured around his head as if he is already preparing for his starring role as a shepherd in the Sunday school Christmas pageant seven or eight years hence.

I can't help but smile looking at him, and I'll have to admit that I've finally gotten to the point in life where I can set aside briefly my male, soldier, macho lunacy long enough to know that it is really okay for a man to allow a tear or two to well up (as long as you lie and say, "Something is in my eye") especially while gazing into the eyes of someone that, for better or worse, has a part of me in him.

There is no way around it. His far-away grandpa can't help but love the little guy.

The strange thing is that I've never met Eli, never seen him, never cuddled him, never held his little hand, never heard him coo or cry. I'm sure he has a good set of lungs as his parents will surely attest.

He was born months after I deployed to the Middle East, long after arriving and enduring the stifling heat of the Iraqi summer, long after LSA Anaconda became home until 365 days of duty in Iraq are completed.

And as sure as I am about anything in life, I know that Eli is loved by this grandpa.

But how? It defies logic. How can a person truly love someone that you've never seen before? Or heard? Or known only from a snapshot on Kodak paper?

All it takes, I discover, is to simply know that he is the child of my daughter and son-in-law, that he is part of my wife's and my family, and that Eli is, indeed, one of us, a part of us.

In my pondering about this wonder of loving Eli, the Christmas story suddenly becomes clearer, taking on a newness I did not have in my fifty-plus previous grandpa-less years.

Could I love someone I had never seen before, never before held in my arms, burped over my shoulder? Someone who up-chucks naturally and without apology all over my clean uniform or clergy collar? Could I love someone whom I had never once gazed upon face to face looking into new, wide, eager eyes?

Can I, indeed, love a God who has never entered my door, looked me in the eyes or verbally spoken, "Someone in eternity loves you"?

Love the Jesus whom I have never touched or beheld, but have only read of by those witnesses or even the witness to the witnesses in the scriptures who have themselves bowed before his manger and laid their gifts before him? Those who have heard his words of mercy for the fallen and disgraced? Sinners like me and every shade and hue in between? Saw and experienced his miracles of healing and forgiveness, touched the scars in his hands and side and have known his mighty, loving presence for the rest of their lives changing them forever?

Can I love such a God and know his love without ever seeing, ever touching him?

Baby Eli, who has yet to speak a word, and his little Christmas tree tell me, "Yes, grandpa. You can."

We look at a thousand manger scenes during our normal holidays in the States and numbly see right past almost every one of them. Here in Iraq with its Islamic dominance there are few such opportunities to overlook the simplicity and power of that scene. But whether we see a crèche here or back home, whether they are stylish and beautiful or cheap, lighted "Made in China" plastic figures on the lawn, we can overcome our desensitized state and still receive the gentle message from eternity announced so strangely through a baby. Look at the Christ Child and see how much God loves you. Listen to the witness of those who first beheld "Emmanuel — God with us" and hear the angel witnesses,

> *Don't be afraid. I bring you good news of great joy*
> *that will be for all people. Today in the town of David,*
> *a Savior has been born to you; he is Christ the Lord.*
> — Luke 2:10-11 (NIV)

A Savior in skin and human flesh, a God who comes to rescue, to save, to bring back all of his wayward creatures into his family?

We don't have to touch the tiny hands, see the soft, pink flesh, or feel the fine hair and warm head of the holy Child against our cheeks to know he is real and to stand in teary, awed amazement at the "... wonders of his love" as the final verse of "Joy To The World" bids us proclaim. To love him without ever laying an eye upon him, we just have to believe the witnesses, gaze at the verbal snapshot of the book and know by faith that he is truly one of us, one of the family, one of God's own. It simply takes a heart willing to receive this child as God's calling card of love, his plan to forgive, to return us to wholeness, to return us to his family, and to bring light and life back to a world living in darkness and surrounded by death.

Yes, we can love someone we have never seen or held before.

Little Eli's beaming eyes peeking through fake, green leaves remind me that God once peeked through the straw of an animal feed trough wrapped not in a soft, terry bath towel, but in the swaddling clothes of a humble human child. And, in that quiet birth in Bethlehem, Almighty God, Wonderful Counselor, the Prince of Peace announces hope to a despairing world, to those wandering in darkness, to those wondering if they are, or can ever be, loved.

The answer from the manger, from the angelic choir, from the Christmas story is a joyous and eternal, "Yes."

Can we love someone we have never seen?

Yes, because that someone has first loved us in a Child who would grow and one day be crucified only to rise again to life, to insure that God's love and presence would forever overcome darkness and death in our lives in Iraq or back home halfway around the world.

"Someone in Iowa loves you," the ornament on the artificial tree proclaims to my weary, aging, pondering, deployed eyes.

This is without doubt true, but it more importantly reminds me of a message the world still desperately needs to hear in the birth of Christ, that "Someone in eternity loves you" as well.

I can believe this good news even in a combat zone, for two babies, one born 2,000 years ago and one brand-spanking-new in 2003 along with a pathetic little tree newly labeled "Eli's Christmas Tree," proclaim the joys and truths of the Christmas story all over again. I never dared dream that an Iraqi windowsill could ever contain, or reveal anew such good news.

Yes, I can love someone I have never seen before; for the Christ Child, Eli my grandson, and the Bible tell me so.

So can you.

Bulk Mailing Or Current Occupant

They came in bulk, lots of them, by the handfuls.

They came with good intentions and the very best of motives, but they lay unopened on the table by the battalion orderly room door for days.

No one seemed interested.

They were Christmas cards written by concerned, caring people in the States. Arriving on New Year's Eve for troops spending Christmas far from home in a strange land, in a combat zone: kindness and concern flowed from every letter and signature.

Labeled "G.I. Joe" or "G.I. Jane" or "A Special Soldier," they still remained unread by the dozen.

Such a shame.

I mused why this was so and the answer was all too clear.

They weren't personal. They weren't cards from someone soldiers knew, cared for, or loved. If it is not from someone they love, then the card doesn't have much impact.

It became apparent that in order for such well wishes to have an impact there must be a personal connection.

"Most Valued Customer" read the ads that come in the foot-thick Sunday paper or one of the multitudes of bulk mailing advertisements that fill our mailboxes back home. (Thankfully that is not something we contend with in Iraq.)

Of course, next to the "Most Valued Customer" printing is our name, often so misspelled that it could have only been created by a heartless computer or someone operating the computer whose native language surely was foreign. Despite such butchering of our intimate monikers, we are still assured that we are most valued and valuable enough to receive this once in a lifetime offer via mail. Then to add insult to injury underneath our valued status appears the completely non-intimate label: "Most Valued Customer Or Current Occupant."

Personal? Warmly intimate and caring? I don't think so. Few do. (But if it is a good pizza deal, it might be worth not immediately dispatching to the garbage.) Valued? Maybe only after the first installment payment of $19.95 is paid.

In our populous and increasingly impersonal world, people need personal connections, not more bulk mailings.

Imagine God sending a generic Christmas card or a bulk message of professed love and peace to his world. "Dear Most Valued Creatures or Current Terrestrial Occupant: I'm here for you. I want you in my family. Best wishes for a happy rest of your life."

Nothing intimate or personal about that.

God could, perhaps, write his greetings in the sky so that the masses could all see at once a cloud spelling, "I love you, world! God."

But all too quickly, scientists would come up with a rational explanation connected to global warming and weather patterns, people would get over the shock of seeing this strange phenomena once they realize the world isn't going to end soon enough and they still have to take out the garbage or wash the dinner dishes. Growing swiftly accustomed to the cloud formation, humans would soon shrug their shoulders over coffee and say, "Did you see that weird cloud the other day?" Then they'd just as quickly move on. "Oh, how are your bunions?" or "When do the kids go back to school?" It might break up the usual weather conversation, but after a while it would hardly be earth shattering or life altering to most people. Lost in the shuffle of everyday living, God's sky message would be seen as less and less awesome and more and more as coldly impersonal. No meaningful connection would be made in the lives of those occupying planet earth.

But head-turning advertising is not God's greatest tool or strategy. He knows this is good only for a certain number of people. His purpose is much bigger and so much deeper than that. His desire is not to grab attention, but to reconnect eternally with his wayward and lost creation on a person-by-person basis.

That's not to say that God is above trying the "signs in the sky" thing. He'll work with most anything to get his offer of a new connectedness with himself to a world too often looking anywhere but at him.

In a way, God has already written messages in the sky for humanity to take note of. He wrote a night sky message to the Magi using the Star of Bethlehem. He also sent angels in the night to scared-to-death shepherds to tell them personally that the humble nobodies of the world get the first shot at witnessing God's glad tidings of great joy.

Yet, ultimately, God knows that skywriting is not the answer.

Something much more intimate, personal, and transforming is needed in human lives. So God sends Jesus, his Son to look us individually right in the eyes and to announce one by one, person by person, "This is how much I love you." God sends his very best to every last person on earth for whom he has good intentions and knows by name, and his best gift of reestablishing a personal connectedness is this baby born in Bethlehem, this Savior, Jesus.

Isaiah, the Old Testament prophet, recorded the intimate plan of God toward his people when he quotes God saying:

> *(1) But now, God's Message,*
> *the God who made you in the first place, Jacob,*
> *the One who got you started, Israel:*
> *"Don't be afraid, I've redeemed you.*
> *I've called your name. You're mine.*
> *(2) When you're in over your head, I'll be there with you.*
> *When you're in rough waters, you will not go down.*
> *When you're between a rock and a hard place,*
> *it won't be a dead end —*
> *(3) Because I am God, your personal God,*
> *The Holy of Israel, your Savior.*
> *I paid a huge price for you...."*
>   — Isaiah 43:1-3 (The Message, a paraphrase)

God proclaims from of old in his word that he already knows us, where we live, work, and play, calls us "by name," and wants a personal relationship of love through the newborn and eventually to-be-crucified Savior who was born in the city of David. This is Christ, the Lord, who would one day in history hang from a cross to free an enslaved world from the guilt and power of sin and then rise victorious to offer us eternity as a gift.

This personal connectedness, of course, is the difference between answering the phone to hear the voice of your best friend or loved one and hearing the voice of a telemarketer calling from

Sheboygan about a new wonderful platinum credit card. God does not call from Sheboygan.

A story that repeatedly reminds me of this personal connectedness is of three young British friends who travelled to Paris and were at Notre Dame cathedral. As young men often do, they got into a dare where one would go to the priest hearing confession and tell him all sorts of horrid stories of sin. One of the young men took the dare and bet, but could not win until after he had done the penance the priest would give.

Off he went into the confessional. The priest listened patiently sensing the joke on him and God. Then he gave the man his penance. He was to go to a particularly life-like statue of the crucified Christ in the cathedral, look into the eyes of Jesus, and say three times, "You died for me and I couldn't care less."

Emerging from the confessional, the young man was not eager to do the penance, but his friends would not let him off the hook. He found the statue of Jesus hanging on the cross in all his agony and sorrow, and looking into the eyes with great hesitation, he said, "You died for me and I couldn't care less."

But something strange boiled up in him as he prepared to look into the eyes of the Christ and say his sentence of indifference again. He hesitated. The eyes of Jesus met his and somehow God was looking through this inanimate object deep into the soul of the young man. Haltingly, he said it a second time, "You died for me and I couldn't care less."

The huge price of God's love for his world, that Isaiah described, struck with full force in the soul of the young man. He could not repeat the statement, lost his bet, and experienced a change in his life that led to becoming a clergyman and eventually an archbishop in the Church of England; all because God stooped to make a personal connection through a dare and a bet.

Eyeball-to-eyeball, soul-to-soul, by name, personal contact with the Son of God is what God is about in this world. For the Lord has paid too high a price to address us in an impersonal bulk mailing or by a generic "G.I. Joe" or "G.I. Jane."

God mostly uses people today to communicate his individual love to others who are yet oblivious or hostile to his presence.

Those who have been freed from their heavy burdens and loads and in gratitude wish to be of joyful use to their Savior can now be the statue of Christ for others to look at and be attracted to. The hands, feet, and eyes of the Savior that attract and welcome the weary, the wounded, the broken, to the person of healing, forgiveness, and intimate wholeness.

In a true miracle of miracles, our Heavenly Father then takes those broken and redeemed sons and daughters and in turn uses them to be the flesh-on-flesh personal connection to those still outside the family of God. He can and will use anything to bring the good news of his love in Christ, but he seems to prefer to use the forgiven, his children of faith and grace in Jesus Christ with names and faces and souls.

So whether it is the Christmas story or the Passion of Christ you hear, always remember the words of the prophet Isaiah of God:

> *... Don't be afraid, I've redeemed you. I've called your name. You're mine.* — Isaiah 43:1 (The Message)

For the God of Christmas and Easter is no bulk mailer.

He wants every last occupant of his world to be known by name and one-on-one to be welcomed into his heavenly, kindly kingdom of love ... no matter if you are a "G.I. Joe," a "G.I. Jane," or a "Current Occupant."

Iraqi Dawn

The early morning had not yet yielded its dawn.

Yet, the vehicles were already lined up bumper-to-bumper in march columns, headlights and radios on, soldiers scurrying as blurred figures in the dark to load last-minute equipment and baggage and to do final vehicle checks.

Weapons and ammunition are one of the last-minute checks, though no rounds would be chambered until the Humvees and Deuce-and-a-halfs rolled out of the concrete and bunkered barriers of the base camp gates.

This is a convoy preparing to depart into the countryside in the dangerous center of Iraq. It is not unlike any of hundreds of other military convoys preparing to depart into the daylight of a cool winter morning of this combat zone. The pre-combat checks are the same, the convoy briefing similar to units all across the hostile theater of operations.

But for this unit, the convoy is different.

The tension is palpable as before all convoys, but this one seems more tense than normal. Everyone knows that the stakes are higher than normal. For this, the unit's last convoy out of Iraq, is the beginning of the long journey home to family, friends, and loved ones.

Soldiers seem eager for the chaplain to come and pray before the mission gets underway.

They have been at war now for almost a year. They are heading home, yet there remains one last journey through the heart of the enemy's homeland that holds plenty of risks. Even the least informed of troops know instinctively that this area holds the most risk. It will be several hours into the convoy before they are outside of the Sunni Triangle and the greatest danger.

Maybe it'd be okay for the chaplain to pray.

All eyes will be glued to the road for the hidden explosive devices that have inflicted the most casualties among American troops. "IEDs" they are called: "Improvised Explosive Devices." Innocent looking roadside litter which blankets the roads of most third world countries can easily harbor a roadside bomb. Animal carcasses, potholes, and road construction can mask the artillery shell that with protruding wires or remote garage door openers or remote toys can ignite the blast that can destroy a thin-skinned Humvee or truck.

It is like looking for a needle in a haystack at 50 mph; difficult, but all will try, as the consequences of missing "the needle" are too deadly.

Perhaps some divine help might be in order. "Chaplain, would you mind praying before we depart? This journey is too important to not make it safely through. We are going home."

Bodies and souls encased in Kevlar and body armor shouldering weapons that have become second nature in the last year bow their heads to pray. Their motivation to pray earnestly is evident and tangible: safety, protection, home.

The chaplain reads from the Old Testament prophet, Isaiah.

> *Israel, the Lord who created you says, "Do not be afraid — I will save you. I have called you by name — you are mine.*
>
> *When you pass through the deep waters, I will be with you; your troubles will not overwhelm you.*
>
> *When you pass through the fire, you will not be burned; the hard trials that come will not hurt you.*
>
> *For I am the Lord your God, the holy one of Israel, who saves you.* — Isaiah 43:1-3 (GNB)

Bowed heads nod in agreement. "Yes, Lord, this is what we ask of you, yet again, in this ancient, troubled, biblical land called Iraq."

These American soldiers at war are mostly young, most without outward interest or expression in religion and faith. Only a handful have been to a worship of any kind in the past twelve months.

For many, their youth has beguiled them into the common notion of those who are healthy and vigorous.

"Surely there are many, many years ahead of me yet, surely there is plenty of time to get serious about God; surely I will not be a casualty."

Even in war, there is the belief that, "Yes, people die, but it won't be me; someone else, yes, but certainly not me."

Human beings are excellent at deluding themselves. "Smoking may cause lung cancer, but not me." "Accidents kill more young soldiers than bullets, but I don't need to wear my seat belt. It won't happen to me." "Yeah, drugs are bad for most people, but I can handle it." And on and on.

But on this cold morning, cracks begin to show in such blind self-confidence.

"Chaplain, pray for us."

Like a supremely confident ball player sitting quietly in the locker room before the big game, the bravado, the self-sufficiency can wane and contemplation yields to more realistic thoughts: "Maybe it could be me today. Maybe my vehicle out of all the dozens of vehicles will be the one hit. God, no! Not now; not today; not going home; this close to making it."

"Pray, Chaplain. We know you have an *in* with the 'Man Upstairs.' Please pray."

Among the wavering, young functional atheists are also those who sincerely believe, but are at differing stages of maturity in the faith.

The least mature believe that the chaplain's words and the cross attached to their dog tags is of sufficient potency to ward off the enemy's attacks much like a cross and garlic repel vampires. (Thankfully, no one chooses garlic to repel the insurgents!)

The more mature and practiced of believers in the knowledge of God understand that words and ornaments are no good luck charms. God is not at the beck and call of incantations, spells, or charms like a rabbit's foot. (As the saying goes, why do you think the rabbit's foot will do you any good? It didn't help the rabbit any!)

No, in praying, the chaplain does not invoke secret formulas for coaxing divine protection out of a reluctant and stingy God.

The prayer is a reminder of the living presence that comes through the love and power of the Savior, Jesus Christ; a presence that promises that no matter what the road outside the gates may hold, he is there with his people.

When you pass through fire, you will not be burned;
the hard trials will not hurt [destroy] you.

— Isaiah 43:2

I will be with you always, to the end of the age.
— Matthew 28:20 (GNB)

"Fire! that's us, Lord, in the Sunni Triangle. Be with us, Jesus. Help us to not be afraid, but to trust you for this and every journey."

The chaplain's prayer is done.

Final instructions are given. The commander and command sergeant major are there to send the convoy off into the faint light of the gathering dawn. Engines roar to life. Radio checks jump across the airwaves and word is passed to "Move out." "Game faces" are put on along with helmets. The lead vehicle passes through the gate. Weapons are put into "red status"; magazines loaded, rounds chambered, and pointed outward toward the enemy.

The journey begins. It must be seen through to its conclusion; there is no other way home.

Safe passage is not guaranteed, but the saving presence is.

"Pray, Chaplain, pray."

How eerily similar this seems to the final moments of the earthly life of the Christian. Family and friends gather at the bedside with the pastor present to pray in the last moments before life's final journey home begins for this child of God; the final journey into the full presence of God.

It is so very near, but has not yet begun for the soldier of Christ who is encased in the Kevlar and body armor of God's love, forgiveness, and salvation. They are prepared despite some pre-journey jitters.

The final prayers of benediction are offered:

Sovereign Lord, as you have promised, you now dismiss your servant in peace.

— Luke 2:29 (NIV)

"Pray, Pastor, pray."

200

The journey through the valley of the shadow of death begins with the safety and light of God's eternal kingdom as its goal.

It is not the pastor or chaplain's words that matter now, but simply the promise of a loving God who tasted danger, suffering, and death on a cross, yet who also brought resurrection and new life to an uncertain, timid, and insecure humanity always immature in its understanding, always prone to wander away from love's sacrifice, yet who always needs to still hear the joy of an Easter morning, "He is not here. He is risen, just as he said."

Prayer is never a good luck charm. In this brutal, dangerous world, God knows we need more than lucky charms. We need words that remind of promises given long ago; promises of the presence, promises that however our journey progresses, the living Savior will bring us safely home to his eternal presence.

"Pray, Chaplain, pray."

"Remind us, Pastor, remind us."

"Do not be afraid — I am with you" in the Iraqi dawn, in the fires and cauldron of all of life's hazardous journeys until by the power and love of God in Christ we are safely and forever home.

The Last Convoy

It sounds rather melodramatic to title anything "The Last."

It smacks of an air of the dramatic, the climatic, as in such films as *The Last Train Out Of Dodge, The Last Picture Show, The Last Action Hero*, or even *The Last Tango in Paris*, where Marlin Brando as his usual bulging self, slithers across the floor with petite young things.

Occasionally the word "last" simply means what it says at its basic, face-value meaning. It is the final convoy in a series of convoys over the course of a year in Kuwait and Iraq. No hidden or symbolic meanings, just the last one.

It will be "The Last Convoy" for a unit of soldiers leaving Iraq and the Sunni Triangle after almost of year of mobilizing for and being involved in the war, otherwise known as Operation Iraqi Freedom.

The motor park of the unit is filled with darkness and the faint images of troops scurrying around in the pre-dawn loading, checking, and waiting for all to gather, organize, and begin.

Sixty-some vehicles in two serials travel this day along with over 130 soldiers, a mixture of active and reserve soldiers. Each has packed loaded duffel bags, food, water, ammunition, and essentials like extra foam cushions to sit on for the long ride in Humvees. The Army rarely spends money for the comfort of ones hindquarters, the Hummer being no exception.

Soldiers waddle through the mud encrusted streets of LSA Anaconda bearing their load to their pre-assigned vehicle in the cool darkness of the early morning. A power grid failure the night before makes the Iraqi morning even more dark and ensures that the sustaining cup of coffee is lacking as coffee makers do not operate without electricity. If there was ever a morning soldiers needed the caffeine ... Kevlar helmets, interceptor body armor with SAPI plates, web gear, and weapons rock rhythmically on their shoulders as they plod toward the motor park.

There is a tension in the air that is more than the chill of a Middle Eastern morning. One would think that there would be nothing but joy in the soldiers who are going home. The joy is there, but is tempered with the knowledge that there is one more task to accomplish. They must convoy through the heart of bandit country otherwise known as the Sunni Triangle.

It is the area of the most resistance to the coalition and the people who had the most to lose when Saddam was defeated. Needless to say, people look upon convoys as targets of opportunity rather than vehicles to wave at.

The apprehension is not constant or severe for most. It is not fear. The occasional rocket and mortar attacks or the news of convoys being attacked that reminds all that this is still war, still a very potentially dangerous place. Stories, real or apocryphal from World War II, Korea, or Vietnam of the soldier killed or wounded on their very last mission before rotating home, or the helicopter that goes down with troops eagerly leaving combat after having survived a year of it, creep into most soldiers' consciousness. These tragedies are not lost upon the psyche of these men and women assembling for their last convoy out of Iraq.

To have made it this far safely, to have survived and endured so much over so many days, only to be wounded or killed in the final hours, well, this is too much to dwell on for very long, yet it is in the back of the minds of many.

Like much of life, the business of living moves forward despite human reservations. The mandatory, pre-convoy briefing is long, rambling, and not well organized by the usually efficient young captain. The dawn is just beginning to break. The unit was assured by the engineers that they will have cleared the roadside mines and bombs commonly known as "IEDs" by the time the convoy moves out the gate. No offense to the engineers, but this seems rather dubious. But dubious or not, it changes nothing. Convoys are on a timetable and we go whether the road has been checked or not.

After a bit of a snafu at the gate over convoy clearance, the unit rolls out the gate, past the protective fence and wire, earthen berms, concrete barriers, bunkers, and guard force.

Metallic clicks punctuate the morning calm as magazines and belts of machine gun ammunition are loaded, rounds chambered, and held at the ready. This is "Weapon Status: Red" — ready to fire except for unleashing the safety switch.

As the convoy reaches its cruising speed of 45 mph, a familiar road outside the gate zooms below the tires. Humvees adjust their interval, not too close, not too far apart as every eye scans the road for suspicious diggings or trash that may have protruding wires, waiting to be detonated from a distance. Even animal carcasses are objects of suspicion as the enemy has used them to hide explosive charges. The Army says that troops find two-thirds of the IEDs before they explode, but no one wants to be in that unfound one-third, so this is considered no time for sightseeing.

The vehicles pass a small village not far from the base where a unit had arranged to refurbish and build an addition to their village school. Several months earlier, a celebration at the school's opening took place there with a festive meal and speeches by the commander, mayor, and Imam.

A master sergeant in the back seat of one Hummer wonders if the heater is on. He can't feel "the love" in the back, it is yet that cool as the convoy soon reaches the four-lane road called "Highway 1."

The anticipation and tension is at its greatest now. This road has been dubbed by some GIs as "IED Alley" because of its frequent attacks on convoys. It is *the* major north-south road leading out of Baghdad toward the Turkish border and very heavily used by both the military and civilians.

Past Taji thirty minutes down the road, another U.S. base that has seen plenty of attacks, the convoy reaches the suburbs of Baghdad and the expansive bridges leading to the northern reaches of the city. We were warned to be very careful here as the enemy had recently been found placing mines in the area.

A large open area of garbage landfill is just to the east, where sheep and people live. It is the same place where, back in May, I saw a young Iraqi girl leading her little flock, when we drove by on our way to Anaconda for the first time. (cf. story: "Recipe") I can still see her in my mind's eye. She wore a bright blue dress, dark head covering and had big, bright eyes. She was smiling, weaving her way through the mounds of garbage and waving at us driving by. I wonder eight months later if she would still be smiling and waving happily at these Americans?

Baghdad overshadows Iraq like New York, Los Angeles, or Chicago overshadows other cities of America. It is the center of attention, and that is not lost on soldiers' minds and consciousness. Sections of the city are calm, in general. Parts are hotbeds of activity and dangerous to American health. Few of us know the city well enough to know which sections are or are not friendly, so we rightly assume the whole route is dangerous.

But, the trip through western Baghdad is uneventful. No one is disappointed. The streets are not crowded, unchoked, unlike when we convoyed through them eight months ago, but it is still relatively early in the morning.

We pass familiar sights, one of Saddam's many palaces now used by the Army, the grand mosque just off the road, the refinery, and the market beginning to fill with fruits, vegetables, and sheep for slaughter along the side of the road. We pass several monuments to the former, now captured, dictator located in the island created by a traffic circle where one can almost, but not quite, see the painted, defaced picture of the tyrant peering out from the plaster wall in the center.

A slight sigh of relief is breathed as the overpasses and exchange leading out of Baghdad are reached, weaving past concrete barriers meant to slow speeding traffic. The six-lane road leading south toward Kuwait lies before the unit. While not out of harm's way, the openness of the area allows flatlander midwesterners from Iowa to breathe a little easier as they can now see their surroundings more clearly.

Down the road we pass familiar sights of roadside Iraqi activity: the palm trees, the villages and houses, some of mud, but others of concrete; the farmers on their little putt-putt tractors heading off to the fields, and the salt ponds evaporating along the highway with their white-laced ground.

We reach our first refueling point called Scania. It has changed significantly since May when it was little more than a roadside pit stop choked with dust. Here is the first recollection we have of palm trees in Iraq as we awoke from our fitful sleep in the early morning by our vehicles after a day of traveling up from our previous home in Kuwait. I remember a rooster with an overactive thyroid, or in the pay of hostile Iraqis, crowing in the dark. More than one tired soldier volunteered to shoot the rooster free of charge, but the convoy commander nixed the combat patrol saying the rooster was just doing his job, albeit with more enthusiasm than was appreciated.

The refueling was fast and efficient and the convoy sped off down the highway again, passing shepherds and flocks while the trees began to thin and the desert began to take over.

Convoy after convoy of other units flowed by as the six-lane interstate allowed for passing on either side. Tensions concerning attacks became less and less with each passing mile, as southern Iraq is far less hostile than the militant center of the country. We see units going north while we travel south. There is a mixture of feelings on seeing them. They are new units, our replacements, and replacements of other Operation Iraqi Freedom-1 (OIF-1) troops. There is a sense of smugness on one hand and a sense of pity on the other.

Smugness in the sense that we look at them and think, "Ha! We're done and you're just starting. We know what it is like and you don't." Then there is also pity. "Yes, we know what it is like and though things will be better for you than it was for us, it will still be a long, dangerous, hot year. We understand. We don't envy you. But, O Lord, are we ever glad to be leaving intact and whole."

It is still blessedly cool as the Humvees pass the changing scenery from palm trees to sparse vegetation. This temperature is so different from the stifling heat of the trip north in May. We detour off the wide, well-paved road to a busier, smaller, two-lane one because Saddam didn't get his interstate completed and the rains of winter made it a mud-infested quagmire.

The drive continues uneventfully apart from several stops for mechanical problems. A tire bounces off one vehicle while fan belts seem to be the problem in another. As with all stops, soldiers exit the vehicles and take up guarding positions on all sides of the convoy. Vigilance is still needed. It is southern Iraq and a much safer area for Coalition forces, but there are also bandits in the classic pirate sense who prey from time to time on convoys, though they usually choose supply trucks with fewer people who are able and willing to shoot back.

The road march resumes. By late afternoon, the night's stop is reached. It is a familiar biblical place. The convoy support center is located virtually next to the ancient city of Ur where the patriarch Abraham, claimed by three monotheistic religions as founder, left for the green pastures of Palestine.

Surely the landscape was far more fertile and verdant 3,000 years ago. If not, it is little wonder why Abraham heeded God's call to leave the place. Apart from it having no snow, there is little that most of us could see as an inducement to want to stay in Ur, Iraq. We refuel our vehicles and I am amused by, and take a picture of, signs next to the refueling point. One states unequivocally "No Smoking." Another states to my amusement "No Urinating on the Fuel Point." I guess that must have been a problem at one time.

The tension of the morning has melted away. We are almost home free and the soldiers can almost taste it. The chow hall serves up good chow as we mingle with units from all over the theater. There are soldiers from the 101st Airborne on their way home from Mosul, like we from Balad, while others are on their way north back into bandit country. A pleasant tent city is available for those passing through with shower and bathroom trailers that actually work and are clean. It is a good omen of things to come as we make our way back to civilization.

The next morning the convoy pulls out of the base's perimeter for the first time in "Weapon Status: Amber," a step down from the normal "Red" of Iraq points north of here. In the cool winter morning, it leaves Ur and Abraham's hometown behind. Like the patriarch, we eagerly leave, but in the opposite direction, for the sands of Kuwait.

The six-lane highway that was rejoined yesterday speeds us toward our final day in Iraq — February 2, 2004. Hours later we pull off onto a two-lane road that joins the border of Kuwait and

Iraq. Poor Iraqi children and some adults beg for food from convoys slowed to a halt by congestion.

The tank ditches, berms, and fences that spread in either direction of the border mean we have now reached the end of Iraqi soil. Still we pass truck after truck, convoy after convoy, heading north with supplies, while also encountering an Italian unit going into Iraq.

We all are so grateful to be heading in the direction we are going and grateful that although we have days of military paperwork, cleaning, and processing to do, we have now left the combat zone of Iraq with all the people the unit started with alive. Although many departed due to medical and other reasons, the enemy did not reduce our number in hostile action as in other units. We are not proud of that as much as just plain happy. So much of the loss in war seems to be mere chance and not due to our being competent soldiers. That may be true, hopefully is true, but the vagaries of combat are too many for anyone to take credit for surviving. Gratitude is the only appropriate response.

In a few more hours, our final Kuwaiti destination is reached.

"The Last Convoy," while undramatic in the annals of military history will, nevertheless, be remembered by these soldiers, if for no other reason than being the final experience of Iraq and a giant step closer to home.

Final Layout

Spread flat upon the cement between the warehouses lodging hundreds upon hundreds of soldiers in wall to wall bunk beds are camouflage rain ponchos.

Platoons of soldiers are in the final stages of the joyful task of redeploying back to American or to friendly shores of any sort. They have been in the Middle East for nearly a year and are more than ready to leave this combat zone called the Central Theater of Operations.

They have been part of, and involved in, the fight to eliminate a vicious dictator and whatever weapons of mass destruction there may be. They did their job well at whatever level and location and now it is time to go home. They are tired after twelve months of 24/7 work and more than ready to leave.

These soldiers have safely exited the ever-present danger of Iraq and are now processing out for the return trip back to loved ones, friends, and the golden lands of flush toilets.

But it is not as easy nor as simple as pulling up to the aircraft in Kuwait, hopping on board, and settling into their seats for the eighteen-hour trip to freedom. Nothing is that simple in the Army.

Mounds of equipment to be turned in must be collected; this includes everything the Army deems necessary to remain in the Theater: body armor, ammunition, and spare field equipment.

Vehicles must be steam cleaned with all residue of Iraq and Kuwait eliminated from every nook and cranny. Inspectors concerned about agricultural contamination are cranky, finicky, and fastidious. In the long run, it will be easier to wash grime off of equipment than washing the Middle East and war out of soldier's minds and lives. But, that is for the readjustment and demobilization period which will be delayed until the equipment is completely clean.

The inspectors don't stop with vehicles. Every departing soldier must have not one, but three complete inspections of all of their equipment, personal and military, that is accompanying them back to the States. Why three is a magical number is anyone's guess, but at least it is biblical.

In the time-honored tradition of soldiering, a layout inspection means all of one's gear is placed on a poncho or poncho liner in some predetermined order and thus open to the scrutinizing eyes of the sergeant or commander.

Every stitch of Army issue or personal clothing is open to view. Is that piece of clothing authorized by regulation? Is it clean? Is it unauthorized, illegal, or considered contraband?

One does not have enough fingers and toes to count the number of times the unit was briefed on what was allowed on the trip home and what was not. Over and over again, soldiers heard the same mantra. At least no one could claim they didn't get the word, at least with any justification.

Your life, your possessions, your underwear, your everything, is laid out and bared for all to see; not just the troops of your unit, but anyone and everyone who walks by heading for the porta-johns and showers. The urge to peruse the personal effects of others is far too much for most normal human beings to abstain from. The inspection can't be avoided; no one, absolutely no one enters the aircraft for home until those three layout inspections are completed.

A complete layout of one's life. Nothing hidden. All bared.

Does this sound like an image, a picture of the judgment day to anyone?

Biblically speaking, there is a day promised where all human beings are to be laid open before God. The exterior images, the facades we have labored so hard all of our lives to create, the glossy and presentable image we want others to see and believe is the real us, all this will be open before God, as well as the parts of us we would rather hide from the gleaming, righteous gaze of our God. The gunk, the garbage we would rather keep buried at the bottom of our soul's inner duffel bag; the contraband of the spirit.

All the good, the bad, and the ugly is laid out on a spiritual poncho at the end of our days before the throne of God. Nothing is hidden. No shell game of deception will succeed in pulling the wool over on the eyes of the Almighty in a vain attempt to keep secret the unsavory, the embarrassing, the real person behind the mask. Humans in their sinfulness usually avoid the piercing light of God and want no one in the universe to see who they really are in the dark.

It is not a terribly comforting thought for most of us to realize that God, and others, are even remotely aware of our spiritual baggage. The words of the pastor in his sermon in the book of Hebrews understand the judgment day and its God all too well:

> *There is nothing that can be hid from God; everything*
> *in all creation is exposed and lies open before his eyes.*
> *And it is to him that we must all give an account of*
> *ourselves.* — Hebrew 4:13 (GNB)

It sounds like a "layout" inspection to a soldier.

The problem is that none of us, no human being, ever has life completely right, never has it "together." No matter how good any life may be or what noble deeds have been accomplished, we all have far more shortcomings, shortsightedness, and downright contraband self-centered sinfulness and evil baggage. The Apostle Paul noted in Romans 2:23, "For all have sinned and fall short of the glory of God."

That falling short, in the Christian understanding, is what brings on a judgment day. Sin is merely a theological way of saying, "We all carry much contraband in our souls; actions, attitudes, and thoughts that in no way honor or please a God of goodness and purity."

A mandatory, final layout inspection before our last journey home to eternity (here God is far more gracious than the Army, reducing the number of inspections from three to just one, but that one carries a whopper of consequences) is not all that comforting a thought for most of us who are aware of our shortcomings. Those who dare to take a fearless inventory of their lives; who they are, where they have been, the baggage of fears, broken trust, and the pettiness they carry, the bodies they have buried on the road of life, are not all that confident of the judgment's outcome. It is enough to make even Mother Teresa quake in her boots.

But there is hope on the horizon for our layout woes.

God, not eager to condemn his creatures, sends his Son to make an appearance at our judgment. He is present because of a relationship of trust and faith that has been established between the Savior and the rebel, a relationship that forgives the obvious and the hidden through the suffering and death of Christ upon the cross. The Savior appears because that is what saviors do, they offer rescue and hope to people sinking in a slew of hopeless baggage; saviors bring life again to the guilty.

Again the Apostle Paul reflects upon this "Good News = Gospel."

> *He [Jesus] rescued us from the power of darkness and brought us safe into the kingdom of his dear Son, by whom we are set free, that is, our sins are forgiven.*
> — Colossians 1:13 (GNB)

It is as if the Christ walks before our laid-out souls; viewing with sadness all that is within his daughters and sons that brings hurt, contamination, and destroys the soul. But, instead of pointing a finger of righteous anger toward the nearest entrance to the fiery world without God, the Lord of the cross sprinkles holy, forgiving blood upon the condemning contraband, the unholy, and the evil, so the revealed uncleanliness is forgiven, cleansed, and removed forever.

This act of completely undeserved love is what a loving God offers to all who are bold and desperate enough to expose their folly and to receive the free gift of a crucified and risen Savior. C. S. Lewis said it well, "Christianity has nothing to offer those who do not believe they are sinners."

But the Christ of Christianity offers life and hope for all who see themselves as they really are and fall at the feet of the Son of God who delights to rescue and free his people from all of their oppressive delusions.

The final layout inspection is done. The baggage is clear and repacked, and the soldier is heading toward the plane that will take them home.

214

The believer, at the end of life, is also cleared and rid of all filth and burdens that could sidetrack their entrance into the kingdom of God. They have been inspected by the Savior who has put his seal of approval on the forgiven child-of-God's head so that, with a smile, Saint Peter waves them inward and homeward at the pearly gates; then the celebration of God's love and mercy and grace kicks into full gear.

> *Then the King will say ... "Come, you that are blessed by my Father! Come and possess the kingdom which has been prepared for you ever since the creation of the world."* — Matthew 25:34 (GNB)

Welcome home, Soldier. No more inspections.

Welcome home, Child of God in Christ Jesus. The final layout is covered in grace and love for all the world to see and for you to rejoice, forevermore.

A Tale Of Two Glasses

This is not one of those optimist/pessimist stories about see-ing the glass either half-full or half-empty.

But it is about seeing, and about seeing with glasses.

Most people below a certain age would rather do anything than wear lenses and frames on their faces and it usually depends upon whether one has hope yet for their looks or, as in my case, has given up on any such miracle. But when you've worn glasses since the seventh grade, with just a few years of contacts, glasses become not just second nature but absolutely essential to every-day living. My eyes are so bad that when I take my glasses off to shave in the mornings, I often have a difficult time locating them again with my natural eyesight, even though they may only be 24 inches from my face.

But, this is not about my appearance or eyesight. It is about two pairs of glasses owned during the war in Kuwait and Iraq. These spectacles are my own civilian wire-rimmed glasses and not the infamous GI labeled birth-control glasses that the U.S. Army favors for its soldiers. (They are called birth-control glasses be-cause they are so ugly that no soldier could presumably ever get a date wearing them.)

One pair of my civilian glasses had been worn through war, sand storms, suffocating heat, and even Iraqi mud splattered from Humvees and trucks. Needless to say, the glasses were scratched in numerous places despite their scratch coating from the optical center.

As Murphy's Law would always dictate, one scratch appeared precisely in my normal line of sight. It couldn't have been more perfectly located if I had used a microscope to situate it in the one place on the lens guaranteed to create the most blurred vision. I don't know how it got there or even when, but it did, and it is there forever and ever.

Such an irritating scratch wouldn't be tolerated very long in normal life. A new lens would have been ordered and put in the frame. Who wants to watch Shrek or the Pink Panther through

217

flawed lenses or gaze at sleeping soldiers during the sermon at worship through such a scratch?

But this is Kuwait and Iraq, and one just doesn't go down to the mall and get a replacement lens. The choice is clear. Either switch to the Army birth-control glasses (not a completely unreasonable choice in a combat zone where looks are the least necessary survival skills for a soldier), or put on your new scratchless ones. Still, a person has to retain some shred of dignity, even in the Army, doesn't he?

There is so much time left in the desert with its sandstorms and it's so easy to lose your glasses in the tent or drop them into the ceaseless muck and mire the shower trailer with big GI feet always available to step on them or grind them into the floor.

Why break out the new glasses so early in the game and take the chance that you'll end up soon with *two* scratched pairs of glasses with no hope of a replacement pair for months?

I decided to get used to the scratch in the first pair and save the good pair for a special occasion like flying home to the States or some such joyous time.

I learned to see around my strategically located scratch. One must occasionally lift up one's head or look down to avoid it, but it can be done. Then, with time, I learned to ignore the other scratches in the lenses wherever they may be, until one day came when I actually removed the glasses from my face and looked at them closely.

I was amazed at how beat up and full of scratches these lenses were after a year of soldiering. Divots were covering the lenses, not just one here or there, but all over. How had I gotten used to them without noticing much at all?

This is a "Tale Of Two Glasses," as I mentioned before. The day finally came when the plane to take us back to the U.S. of A. was right before us in the Kuwaiti afternoon. My moment had arrived and out of the backpack holding my essential-to-life items like candy and pop tarts (never assume the Army is going to feed you on time), out came my new, scratch-free spectacles. Same style gold wire frames, but with lenses as pure and smooth as a newborn baby's bottom.

I put them on my old, desert-tanned, aging face and immediately the world seemed brighter, clearer. No more sight-altering scratches to peer through or around; just plain, fresh, clear light. While not as dramatic, this change might be compared to the difference between looking into the muddy waters of the Mississippi and a clear, blue Oregon mountain stream.

The Christian faith has been described as an experience of putting on a new life, new garments, new wineskins, new yeast for leaven, new birth, a new heaven and a new earth, a new covenant, a new Jerusalem, a new name, a new lots of things, but there are no new glasses. Yet it isn't a big leap to imagine Jesus in an age of spectacles saying, "Behold, I make all eyes new. I bring a new way of seeing God and the world" (based on Revelation 21:5).

Or we can hear the words of Saint Paul describing the essence of an encounter with the crucified and risen Savior:

> *So if anyone is in Christ, there is a new creation: everything old has passed away; see, everything has become new!* — 2 Corinthians 5:17 (NRSV)

Suddenly, with a new set of peepers, the plane on the Kuwaiti tarmac, the bald spots on the head of the old soldier sitting in the seat before me, and the spots on my desert uniform after a year of wear were all more clear than ever. A new set of glasses makes a tremendous, joyful difference!

I believe that is what it means to be in relationship with Jesus Christ. Whether the encounter is swift and dramatic or slow-cooked over time, God, in Christ Jesus, plans to give us all new sight. Many times Jesus healed the blind. His mission as the Messiah was to bring a new life and sight to a humanity so blinded by its own self-centeredness and self-absorption that it could see no one but its own interests and ways. Classically called sin, this sight-obstructed way of life led only to pain and destruction.

But God, in his love, deigned that he would send his Son as the rescuer of the blind and restorer of new sight.

The new Christian, in his baptism, puts on this new life and sight, seeing Jesus from a perspective the eyes of those outside of his dominion cannot experience. It is perhaps why the hubbub over the movie *The Passion of the Christ* is so intense; those who object to the violence and its graphic portrayal seem to object because they see no redeeming value in Jesus' death.

It is pure injustice done violently to a good, kind teacher, but he is no more than a rabbi, then the vivid portrayal of such suffering is little more than gratuitous Hollywood violence, like sequel upon sequel of *Rambo* or *Terminator* movies.

But the new eyes of faith look upon the agony of Jesus as somehow redemptive, a way God wins us back from the power of evil eyes that capture us so surely in our sinfulness. The sacrifice of Jesus coupled with the resurrection of the Christ frees a world chained in defiant slavery to become beloved children of God who see more clearly than at any time in their lives, a sight that brings newness, hope, and healing.

It is seeing the redemptive suffering and powerful defeat of sin, death, and the power of evil that bring us to the foot of the cross and to the rolled away stone at the tomb with mouths utterly agape at God's actions on our behalf and in that moment of simple confession, "Jesus is Lord. Jesus is *my* Lord." The scratchy, blurred glasses fall away and a new pair are lifted to our eyes where God will see that they stay through thick and thin, through trial or tribulation, for we belong now to him forever.

Life is a tale of two glasses.

One pair is scratched beyond repair. The other is new, unspoiled, and eternal.

We know which pair God, in his love and grace, desires all of his children to wear this day and always.

Lord Of The *Redeployment* Ring

Perhaps you are not a fan of *The Lord Of The Rings Trilogy* and have neither read the books nor seen the movies.

But, if you are and have seen the final movie, *Return Of The King*, then perhaps you could understand the perfect visual illustration of soldiers' redeployment emotions after a wartime deployment.

The Lord Of The Rings is at its essence an adventure story in a classic war movie genre. It is a story about life's eternal combat between good and evil, the seduction and possessive destructiveness of power for self, and the goodness of power denied for the sake of all; a tale of the struggle, sacrifice, and devotion of characters whose contributions, whether small or pivotal, whether knowingly or unknowingly, are essential to the triumph of good in the final battle.

The four books and three films of J. R. R. Tolkien's *The Hobbit* and *The Lord Of The Rings* navigate through the twists, turns, victories, and defeats of the Hobbits (short human-like beings with amiable lives, big feet, pointed ears, and voracious appetites), elves, humans, and wizards of Middle Earth who must summon enormous courage to pursue the relentless battle for the good and safety of others in the face of impossible odds and toiling, terrible struggle.

The *Trilogy* reveals how the greatest warriors are often not the strongest of body, but the stoutest of heart; that the smallest and most docile ones are the very heroes upon whose fate Middle Earth (and maybe our world?) can and does depend.

It is a great adventure story of overcoming horrendous obstacles and odds. The journey to destroy the ring of overwhelming power is long, arduous, twisting, and exhausting. Just watching one of the *Lord Of The Rings* movies in an evening is more than enough, much less tackling all three in one overnight setting. They are long movies to sit through for those with hemorrhoids or bad backs, but it is worth the sit, no matter what the sacrifice, for in the end, good triumphs, albeit at a great price, and in the end all is well with the world. Or is it?

In the waning moments of the final film, the Hobbits, the acclaimed heroes of the titanic struggle, return home to the "Shire," in the anticlimactic epilogue. Back in this quiet, pastoral land of Middle Earth, Frodo, the main hero, and his three supporting companions sit in a tavern with the normal Saturday night celebrations of other Hobbits going on all around them.

There is a loud, partying atmosphere in the tavern, but the four war veterans sit by themselves quietly at a table with their ale, staring uncomfortably at each other. They seem unable to join in with the frivolity of the other Hobbits.

They had been through so much together, through so many struggles, so many fears and obstacles that seemed impossible to overcome and now, upon their return, sitting quietly amidst the surrounding banter, the truth is painfully obvious to them and them alone. Their fellow Hobbits have been and still are oblivious to the frightening and numbing battle that raged in the world all around them. They could not, even if they recognized their deficiency, begin to comprehend the experiences of the four Hobbits sitting in their midst.

Unable to join in on the revelry, Frodo and his friends could not possibly hope to share their adventures with their fellow kinsmen, for few seem to care, and even fewer could identify with their life-changing experiences. The Hobbits can only look at each other, each understanding this same lonely truth. The silence spoke volumes as each understood there was little left to say.

Eventually, Frodo realizes he has been so changed by the adventure that he can identify with it and little else and chooses to sail off into a world so different from the ways of the Shire that he will never return.

The other Hobbits, after a sad, painful process of saying goodbye to Frodo and letting go of the adventure, return home to eventually readjust to life in the Shire nearly as it was in the days before the battle. They are certainly changed and different, but somehow are able to move back into their old lives and world.

Reading the books or watching the movies may be a big price to pay for those not enamored by a fantasy world of courage, danger, and adventure, but for those who do, contemplating the final movie's epilogue can provide an emotional feel for veterans of any struggle, battle, or war where the stakes are high. In our highly visual society, this ending can portray, perhaps, the emotions and thoughts of soldiers of all wars, most recently the war in Iraq or Afghanistan.

Few, except other veterans, can fully understand what it was like and how the soldier can feel so alone even in a crowded tavern surrounded by numerous merrymakers. Family members, no matter how eager and hard they try to understand, just can't bridge the chasm. It's like a husband trying to understand the pain of his wife in childbirth. Sympathetic, yes. Fully comprehending, no. Never can, never will.

Soldiers, as well as family members, need to understand this and simply accept. The radically different experience of war insures that those and only those who have been through it in some similar circumstance can ever truly identify to one extent or another.

Family members can best serve their soldier by actively listening, asking questions, and accepting that they cannot fully digest what their loved one has been through. And that is simply okay. The husband can appreciate, but never fully understand, the pain and joys of childbirth; the same is true of the family of their soldier.

OIF (Operation Iraqi Freedom) soldiers, like the veteran Hobbits of the *Lord Of The Rings*, have been changed because of the past year. Yet, most of the rest of society notes this only in passing brevity as they go about their normal, everyday business. Iraq is an item on the daily news, but life in Iraq and concern for those still engaged there seems to be far from average reflection.

The stay-behind Hobbits who never left the Shire are truly oblivious to the four companions who have shared struggle, danger, and the presence of death. They, in turn, sense they can only be understood and find solace in each other. Is it any wonder then, that especially for past generations the American Legion and Veterans of Foreign Wars are organizations that appealed to those who have seen war and survived it? Who else can understand and identify but another veteran?

Yet the good news in this, as in the movie, is that the Hobbits, and most returning soldiers, do adjust with time and understanding to a life similar, but different to what they knew when they left for war. Change does that to all, whether on the war front or the home front.

So when you watch *The Lord Of The Rings: The Return Of The King*, keep your eyes alert after the climax of the battle of good versus evil. That is easy to spot with the final battle and the awarding of honor to the heroes.

But before you start feeling for your coat and gloves in the dark, pause long enough to watch the tavern epilogue. As you do, think about the 130,000 active and reserve soldiers returning from Iraq and Afghanistan and consider the difficult, but inevitable requirement of redeployed soldiers to reorient their minds and emotions from war to peace, from what they have seen and done overseas to a society they once knew before battle, but may seem so very different now.

Your nonjudgmental communication, openness, and listening are the keys to the power of the "Lord of the *Redeployment* Ring" and the readjusting of U.S. soldiers, your spouses, friends, and neighbors.

SRP Blues

A surlier bunch could hardly be found outside of prison walls.

They sat in bleachers inside a gym with no tense rivals before them on the basketball court in a make-or-break, bragging-rights game. In fact, the court was filled, not with basketballs and sweaty athletes in expensive Air "somebody famous" shoes, but with desks, signs, and chairs.

Before the soft-spoken female sergeant sat soldiers, just 24 hours removed from the Middle East back to America for the first time in over a year, a year of war or as the Army calls it, "Stabilization Operations."

These reserve soldiers had had enough of the active Army and were on their way home. But the administrative processing called "The SRP" stood in their way. A year of endless military paperwork and long lines had given them a very low tolerance for inefficiency.

And this gaggle seemed to be military inefficiency at its finest.

One would think that soldiers just back from war would be all smiles, would be pleased with being out of Iraq and Kuwait, and would consequently display a jovial tolerance of all things trivial.

One would think....

But, whatever good will there might have been in this situation was quickly squandered by the Army. The word to soldiers on arrival at the demobilization site was, "Tomorrow are medical physicals and blood draws. No eating, drinking, or alcoholic beverages after 1800 hours tonight."

This was not well received.

After soldiers were forbidden alcoholic drinks for almost a year, imbibing was almost considered a sacred, inalienable right. The implied consequence of disobedience was a long delay in returning to home station, which caused few attitudes to rise above crash levels, although few were willing at this point to call the Army's bluff. So the unit went dry.

Half the soldiers were to be on the bus the next morning at 0445 hours for the aforementioned blood draw. Jet-lagged and decidedly not thrilled by such an early hour, soldiers shrugged it off as just another day in the Army.

The next morning, compliant, dry troops gathered on cold buses for the ride over to the medical clinic for the physical examination. In the mid-February midwest, it was still and completely dark.

However, true to Army form, someone failed to alert the medical unit at Fort Riley, Kansas, that on a President's Day holiday weekend, a unit returning from a combat theater would be awaiting their blood draw at 0500 hours, in the cold, in the dark, and with even darker attitudes.

Experiencing cold that didn't exist in their desert year, with growling stomachs reporting noisily from all over the packed bus, the troops were informed that the required fast, the abstention from food and drink was, in fact, in error. It was not necessary and nothing could be done on the out-processing until 0800. The Army's "Stealth Joy Killers" had struck again.

That is why even normal skeptical attitudes and surly scowls toward the military were at all time highs in the bleachers that morning.

Those in charge and giving briefings on the SRP process before the soldiers had a tough crowd to work, a crowd that in returning from a war zone was even less likely to accept Army inefficiency with grace and understanding. Their cup of such was filled to overflowing.

SRP is another glorious military acronym meaning "Soldier Readiness Processing" which seems to be a nice way of announcing "Red Tape Distributed Here."

Numerous medical and administrative stations dotted the gym floor, checking everything from shots to pay records. Blood was drawn (but full stomachs were acceptable), needed shots were given, surveys filled out, teeth checked, and hearing tests given. This process had also been in place as the unit had left for their tour of duty.

Since the process consists of navigating through all the stations using a required checklist, long lines at each station are more the norm than the exception.

Sporadic outbursts of grumbling filled each station as processing directions were not clearly given and confusion reigned. Attitudes continued to fall from their already low levels despite some soldiers getting the chance to eat chow. The growling stomach noise level subsided somewhat.

The stabilizing force that keeps soldiers from going "postal" through these frustrations is both a lack of means (for example, weapons and ammunition) and the knowledge that unless this process gets accomplished, there is no homecoming; the eagerly awaited homecoming with spouse and family.

Like soldiers around the world who have throughout the ages stood in innumerable lines, these Iraqi veterans just shut up (somewhat) and did what was required. It is the duty of a soldier to do so.

The day drags on, the checklist slowly receives its approving initials, attitudes slowly rebound as the list is accomplished and the final station with the authority to release the soldier arrives.

We've all had similar experiences with institutions of every stripe, from license stations to tax bureaus, to college registration lines.

Unfortunately, many equate a relationship with the Almighty along the lines of an SRP checklist. God becomes a "SRP God" or a "Checklist God."

It is as if in humanity's relationship with the divine, what really matters is not the conversation with, or love for God, but merely a matter of getting through some heavenly mandatory checklist. Playing the part of a surly bunch in the bleachers, humanity sees God merely as someone who requires certain requirements to be accomplished before heavenly bliss can be granted. The checklist is for our good and is unbendingly rigid in its requirements.

No checklist, no homecoming. Period.

From Islam to Judaism to Christianity and 1,000 variant strains in between, the notion that one must follow the rules, get a list checked off, do this, do that, is prevalent and once that is accomplished, then, and only then, can eternal bliss be a possible consideration.

Avoid the list and eternity may be terminated or as in Hinduism, you keep going around and around life going up or down in the reincarnation cycle until you get the good list accomplished.

But the checklist-God that extremely conservative evangelical Christianity proclaims is least like the God that Jesus revealed.

Although Christians have always innately attempted to add an SRP station here, an SRP station there, add a requirement here and a requirement there for a true relationship with God, Jesus and the New Testament witness do not. Saint Paul states:

> *For through faith, and this is not your own doing; it is the gift of God, not the results of works, so that no one may boast.* — Ephesians 2:8, 9 (NRSV)

The Christian faith at its core is not about dos and don'ts, lists and checklists, and fasts or feasts. It is about looking God in the eyes through his Son, Jesus Christ, and acknowledging that no matter how many times I go through the stations, or fill out my checklist, I can never get them *all* right. If my eternity depends on my doing the list perfectly, then I am doomed to an eternity of standing in line at one hopeless station after another and it never, ever will change.

But instead of such hopelessness, the Savior appears and promises to all in the prison of an endless SRP-legalism, that he has come to

> *... bring good news to the poor, proclaim liberty to the captives, recovery of sight to the blind and to set free the oppressed and to announce that the time has come when the Lord will save his people.*
> — Luke 4:18, 19 (GNB)
> (Jesus reading from Isaiah)

On the cross, Jesus fulfills our checklist, our requirements, our punishment for continued, sustained failure before God, and in the resurrection, he offers up a new relationship, that of becoming one of God's own family, a son or daughter of God.

No surly bunch standing in line only begrudgingly, but children of God, rejoicing in the freedom, forgiveness, and gift of God in Jesus Christ.

Christians have a choice: Faith in a checklist to make it to eternity's shores, or faith in a person, a Savior offering no lists, no boasting, no obligations except to love. In that listless life, the only response is love and gratitude for the gift purchased at the price of Jesus' blood, sacrifice, and passion.

Let the Army do what it must with their SRP list. There are no SRP Blues for those who trash their checklists with God.

Knowing that is what God intends, we can celebrate, here and now, anticipating the homecoming awaiting us at our eternal home where there will be no bleachers filled with surly soldiers, only members of God's family of forgiveness and love.

The Stranger And Ben Hur

I've had some experience with being a stranger, lately.

As a chaplain and soldier mobilized for war in Iraq, the military virtually guarantees that my travels will take me to places unknown and far from home. This, in turn, guarantees that obstacles will be "front and center" when seeking out a local place of worship to hear the Word of God and to receive Holy Communion.

Most of these obstacles are of local vintage, although each church has its own unique way of creating them. Unless the congregation is composed of highly mobile believers who have experienced the same uncertainty of finding, and connecting, to a church in unfamiliar territory, most members seem oblivious to the difficulties of a "seeking" stranger.

Our Army Reserve unit had just landed back in the good ole U.S. of A. on Valentine's Day after a year in Kuwait and the Sunni Triangle of Iraq. We were being processed to be demobilized at one of the active Army's military posts in order to return back to our homes and civilian lives.

The unit had finished the process and departed a few days earlier to a welcome-home ceremony before 800 cheering family members, relatives, and friends. Walking in before those clapping, cheering throngs and spying in the crowd loved ones that we hadn't seen in over a year and during war had wondered if we'd ever see again, was a once-in-a-lifetime wonderful experience.

I suppose that experience was akin to what WWF wrestlers or heavyweight boxing champions hear every time they enter the ring. But most of us non-celebrities and mere mortals can rarely, if ever, expect such a welcome in our lifetime.

Alas, for some it could not last, as we were medical holdovers; soldiers who had medical issues to be resolved before the Army released us back to civilized civilian life. Thus, we were not back home to stay and had to return to "Fort Far-Away-From Home" until they were fixed.

The contrast, then, of the welcome-home ceremony with my Ash Wednesday experience seemed that much more exaggerated, being separated by a mere week. Ash Wednesday found me at

"Fort Far-Away-From-Home" with no home unit, few familiar faces, and even fewer soldiers of a Protestant persuasion who had the tradition or inclination of attending a mid-week service during Lent, the season of focus on the suffering of Jesus and Christian discipleship.

Thus, flying solo, I went in search of a place of worship to hear the traditional words and theme that begins the season of Lent: "Remember that you are dust and to dust you shall return." In remembering this, I also needed to receive in Holy Communion the assurance that despite being dust (aka a dirtbag), the Almighty, in his love, still calls me his redeemed child of God in Christ Jesus.

It wasn't so easy to find those words and gifts in worship. In fact, even as a chaplain and pastor, it was frighteningly easy to give in to the rationalization that staying put in the room on this dark, winter night and watching *Ben Hur* on television was almost as good as attending worship, although "Ben" did not offer Communion.

In overcoming this temptation, the first challenge was attempting to find an Ash Wednesday service on the military installation. Going to a chapel, I discovered that there were, in fact, three services, but they were all for Catholic believers and absolutely none for Protestant Christians. Strike number one.

"When at first you don't succeed, try, try again."

The next try was to look for off-post or civilian services. The phone book's "Yellow Pages" section is the simplest way to find if any of your long-lost relatives live in the area and to find churches that may offer an opportunity to worship.

Ah, so simple! Right? Wrong!

Recorded phone messages should be an effective method of disseminating important information to the stranger. The members of the congregation don't need to listen to find out this information. They usually have a bulletin or newsletter or another church friend to call in order to find out the details that may have escaped them. Not so with the stranger.

But few of the recorded messages did the job. Christmas schedules, no matter how appropriate to December, help little at the beginning of Lent. Most had Sunday schedules intoned with dry, "read the script" voices, but few mentioned current special or mid-week services. The result? I knew there was a church, what their times of Sunday worship were that I didn't need to know, and I still didn't know if there was an Ash Wednesday worship service or not.

Sigh. This is becoming too much like the Army; trying to discover common, readily available information that somehow becomes buried hidden treasure. The search becomes a frustrating maze of false avenues and dead ends where no information or useless information is the result.

Ben Hur was looking more and more like a viable, spiritual Ash Wednesday alternative.

Searching for a congregation of my denomination, I discovered none locally, yet two weeks later, in the daylight, when I drove to the church I had finally settled on, I came across such a church. For some reason it was unlisted in the "Yellow Pages" and invisible to the complete stranger.

Finding an unfamiliar church in an unfamiliar town is a difficult enough chore without also adding darkness to the situation. On a dark Ash Wednesday evening, it is almost impossible to identify a church with a small, unlighted sign.

Only the faint rays of a streetlight enabled me to catch the name and denominational heritage of the darkened church, but even at that, the lettering on the sign was too small to distinguish any worship times.

A reasonable question at this point would be: "What incentive would anyone other than an absolutely determined stranger have to worship here?"

Little, if any. It was almost as if the church was a country club where only insiders with information were welcome. Somehow, I doubt that is the message of the gospel.

The strange thing was that after worshiping elsewhere, I returned by that church which was now populated with numerous vehicles and had lights burning. They had had some Ash Wednesday event after all, but to the seeker this was an unknown mystery. How could one not conclude that this was not a welcoming place despite what would be certain denials of such intent from those gathering therein?

Ben Hur would have to wait as I did find a congregation that was having an Ash Wednesday service, though not of my own denomination. Still, they were close enough for "government work" as the saying goes, and they did all the simple welcoming and informational tasks right.

Their phone message was simple with worship times near the beginning of the recording rather than at the end of a long list of friendly blather. The message even informed me about the special Ash Wednesday service.

The lighted sign enabled the searcher to identify the structure easily even traveling down an unfamiliar street at 35 mph in the dark. It also announced that evening's service and time. The sign and lighted church signified, "We are open for business and are glad you found us."

Many congregational members are afraid of approaching an unfamiliar face in their church and usually don't, but upon entering, a kind elderly lady greeted me almost immediately asking if I was a visitor — another good sign. The pastor was greeting parishioners by the sanctuary entrance and the ushers were doing their jobs of welcoming and directing.

From a similar faith group, but different denomination, I asked if I was welcome to take communion during the service. It had become more important than ever, while at war, to receive the Lord's Supper at every worship and I had not had the opportunity to do so for weeks now as the transient nature of our unit's homeward movement precluded all opportunities to receive God's grace in the bread and wine. This Ash Wednesday, I looked forward to it, but was uncertain if I was welcome to do so, due to my differing denominational affiliation.

My fears were, in fact, rewarded.

An usher directed me to the pastor to answer my uncertainty. When learning of my return from Iraq and church affiliation, he was amiable, but then informed me that he could not in good conscience offer me the Lord's Supper. He offered to discuss the reasons why later, but being demobilized left me with no long-term plans to stay in the area, so I declined. I had heard all I needed to know. I was not welcome at the Lord's Table except under their terms. That was fair, but disheartening.

Disappointed, but not completely surprised, I could do nothing but think, "Well, Lord, I tried. I really tried. Maybe I should have settled for *Ben Hur* and the television." Still, I decided to stay and at least hear the Word of God anyway, on this start to the Christian season of emphasizing repentance.

That was my noble intention, but I must confess that although the sermon was good, my mind could not concentrate on any thought for very long before returning to my exclusion from the Lord's Table. Theologically and in church policy, I understood perfectly well the reasoning. But emotionally, I could not help but reflect upon on how different the response would have been in a tent in a combat theater, in a much more dangerous place than the polished beauty of this peaceful sanctuary in America.

In war, the urgency of the message of grace trumped the differences that separated me now from the altar rail and the pew I sat in; the differences that somehow seemed so much more small and inconsequential compared to being shot at and possibly being grievously wounded or killed. Those differences were subordinated to the need to enable access to all who desired to hear and touch God's grace in the word and the sacrament. I was welcome up to, but not including, the altar; into the sanctuary, but not to the sacrament. My mind understood, but my heart could not comprehend.

While sadly meditating on my return to the denominational divisiveness of normal church life, I also realized that no one in the pews around me seemed to notice that as a stranger I might need help navigating through the bulletin and liturgy. This is a common fault of congregations and leaves a definite unwelcoming impression.

While the liturgy may be familiar to them on Sunday, it can be a challenge for both the initiated as well as the uninitiated in a special, once-a-year worship like Ash Wednesday. The bulletin was clear and uncomplicated, but a stranger will almost always benefit from a handshake, a smile, and a personal touch of help in an unfamiliar situation.

When no one expressed concern that someone in the pew next to them might be lost liturgically, another unintended message was unspoken, but just as real. It was a message of apathy that the stranger might also be lost spiritually and seeking hope. Welcoming the stranger and communicating the welcome of the Savior go hand in hand.

So the overarching unintended consequence of these actions and non-actions by these congregations toward the foreigner amongst us seems to add up to be: "You got here on your own, despite our best efforts to keep you in the dark and now that you are here, we intend to still keep you in the dark. You are on your own. You'll get no help from us. *Ben Hur* might have been a better choice this Ash Wednesday. Besides, we aren't all that sure about the liturgy ourselves."

We live in a culture where the vast majority of people would not even go beyond the most cursory attempt at finding a place to worship; and while discipleship or following Jesus is not life's easiest path, finding a welcoming church should not be difficult, either.

It is the task of each congregation, and each member thereof, to look around and imagine themselves to be a foreigner in a strange place and to ask, how would I go about finding my church, the times and special circumstances of worship? If I was completely unfamiliar with my church's worship routine, how would I find help, who would help me, who has their spiritual binoculars on to spot the lost, liturgically, and perhaps, even spiritually?

Assume nothing is a good piece of advice for the regulars, the initiated, those seeking to be true evangelical (sharing good news) Christians.

I did get to see *Ben Hur* after all, despite my self-denial of the classic on Ash Wednesday. Several days later, all alone in my room, tears streamed down my face at the death of Jesus and its healing of Juda ben Hur and his family. The movie climaxed with the blood from the Savior flowing down the cross into a running stream of water down Golgotha as the violent storm of nature cried out at the Savior's unspeakable death.

The blood and water of God's forgiveness and love in his Son mix and cascade down Calvary, spreading to more and more streams; a visual image of the welcoming and spreading grace of God to a desperate, lonely, lost world.

My tears also flowed that churches nearly 2,000 years later still, intentionally or unintentionally, make it difficult for the water of life and the healing blood of the Savior to flow to the stranger in their midst.

Come to think of it, maybe *Ben Hur* would have been the easier and more redeeming choice on Ash Wednesday.

> *I was a stranger and you received me....*
> — Matthew 25:35 (GNB)